EVASION
and
REPATRIATION

Slovene Partisans
and Rescued American Airmen
in World War II

M000300548

John Rucigay Story
on Page 81

George Mc Govern's Story
on Page 184

Former runner up for President

Johns Friend Joe Maloney's
Story on Page 43

VASION
and
REPATRIATION

*Slovene Partisans
and Rescued American Airmen
in World War II*

Edi Šelhaus

unflower University Press ®

1531 Yuma (Box 1009), Manhattan, Kansas 66502-4228

© 1993 by Edi Šelhaus

Printed in the United States of America on acid-free paper.

ISBN 0-89745-161-9

Edited by Julie Riley Bush

Layout by Lori L. Daniel

Contents

Preface

During World War II, Yugoslavia was the only country in Europe in which small partisan units joined together and liberated their homeland. This armed force, the National Liberation Army of Yugoslavia, closely cooperated with the Allies in their joint war effort. Among the many operations supporting their common fight against the enemy in Europe was the rescue and repatriation by the Partisans of airmen shot down over Yugoslavia. The Yugoslav people helped these airmen because they believed that an alliance against aggression without distinction of nationality, language, or color would engender a spirit for a brighter future for mankind.

I initiated this book as a private citizen of Yugoslavia without government assistance. My goal was to preserve the human experiences and relationships developed as a consequence of the help provided by the Partisans and civilians to American airmen during World War II.

I served as a photojournalist with the Partisan forces during the war. I have authored several photo-histories and have written two books on repatriated Allied airmen.

Some years ago, while I was a photojournalist preparing material for one of the larger Yugoslav newspapers, *Delo,* I learned of a story appearing in a women's magazine with a large circulation that concerned an American B-17 Flying Fortress that had crashed in the southwestern part of Slovenia, a republic of Yugoslavia, in March 1944. It seemed very interesting and worth further research. While some of the crew members perished, the villagers mentioned that some had been rescued. How they were rescued, by whom, and what had become of them were questions that I wanted answered. I invited the readers to write to me about the event, and the response was overwhelming. I received interesting data about similar cases from all over Slovenia, and they all had something in common: the date of March 19, 1944.

I concluded that the date must have been one of the most horrible days experienced by the United States 15th Air Force. Within the territory of Slovenia occupied by the Germans, several B-17s and B-24s had crashed on their return flight from Germany. However, I could not check or verify any of the data until after I retired.

One of the documents that helped me on my quest was a list of the American airmen rescued in Slovenia: "Allied Airmen and Prisoners of War Rescued by the Slovene Partisans," published by the Research Institute Ljubljana (Yugoslavia) in 1946. It identified the names, ranks, locations, and the like of 305 American personnel who were returned to their bases from Partisan airstrips during the period of January 30, 1944, through March 31, 1945. Since the aggregate for all of Yugoslavia was much greater and required extensive travel over a larger area, I decided to concentrate on the events that occurred within Slovenia.

I was most interested in the initial encounters, when the success or failure of the rescued and the rescuer was determined by timing. In many cases, a hundredth of a second resulted in eluding mortal danger and concluded in a happy ending. Unfortunately, the opposite was also true.

It also was important to me that everyone who participated in offering assistance to the airmen be remembered: children, women, and villagers in addition to the Partisans.

In order to validate the authenticity of the data received, I visited the village of each letter writer, surmising that each witness would recollect the events of 35 years past in his or her own way. There were numerous cases where nameless individuals had risked their lives to help the airmen hide from the Gestapo. They had treated the airmen and nursed and encouraged the wounded until they fully recovered and were able to travel and evade the German outposts on their journey to the Partisan airstrips.

All of the stories were initially published as articles in several newspapers. However, as a result of an experience in Kobarid, I felt that they should be compiled and published in book form. I took a picture that is rare even for an experienced photographer: Decades after the war ended, I witnessed the first reunion of a Slovene farmer and an American businessman, Bill Petty from Tennessee, as they embraced. I was so impressed by the spontaneous reaction at that moment that I was determined to write a book with the symbolic title *Stotinka Sreče (One-Hundredth of Luck).* The book was published in 1980 and was quickly sold out.

Public reaction to the book was unexpectedly great. Since I was deluged by mail with new material that included numerous details, I requested the assistance of Janez Žerovc, an instructor pilot operating from the Lesce (Bled) airport in Slovenia. Together we sorted all of the new material that had not been included in the book. We were successful in contacting many individuals who helped clarify the events seemingly lost in history.

We also were aided in our search by an American, John Hribar, as we prepared the material for a second book with the same theme. John was a history buff who served with the U.S. Marines and was wounded on Iwo Jima. He was also interested in the heritage of his parents, who had immigrated to the USA before World War I. Writing to several U.S. veterans' organizations, he succeeded in locating a few of the American airmen assisted in Yugoslavia, a task that had eluded me for several years. Among them was pilot John Merritt, whose crew was rescued by the civilians and Partisans in the area of Koprivnica. His aircraft was nicknamed *Liberty Belle*. When Merritt later visited the site where his plane had crashed, he whispered, "Good-bye, *Liberty Belle,*" which was the inspiration for the title of my second book, *Zbogom, Liberty Bell,* published in Slovenia in 1988.

Shortly afterwards, I flew to the USA to visit some of the airmen whose fate I had been researching for more than ten years. I gave them copies of the book — unfortunately for them written in the Slovene language — which described their experiences. It was clear from their comments that the collection of stories from both books should be translated into English for the benefit of the American public in general and the American airmen and their families in particular.

My wish is to document a memorable period of humanity, assistance, and comradeship between the Slovenes — the people who live on the sunny side of the Alps in northwest Yugoslavia — and the American airmen who shared their fate under dramatic circumstances during World War II.

My main objective is to preserve the precious bonds between peoples for future generations.

Acknowledgments

I wish to express special thanks to Janez Žerovc, who coauthored several of the stories and without whose assistance this book would not have been possible. He helped research a great many leads provided by the subjects of this book and engaged in field trips to verify many of the facts given by the participants. His command of the English language was especially beneficial, as was his expertise in the field of aviation, in which he is a licensed pilot for both powered aircraft and sailplanes. He is Slovenian and currently resides in Kranj, Slovenia.

Many thanks are also bestowed on Svantevita (Vitka) Kolar, who resides in Ljubljana, Slovenia. Vitka translated each story from Slovene to English, typing the original double-spaced draft on manuscript paper.

I also wish to express gratitude to two Americans of Slovene heritage, John Hribar and John Rucigay, for their invaluable aid and assistance. Hribar was my initial contact in the USA. He was instrumental in locating all of the American airmen whose stories appear in this book and transmitting their recollections to me. He placed notices in veterans' magazines and wrote scores of letters to individuals and organizations across the USA during the many years that he was associated with me. He visited me in Yugoslavia and also participated in discussions regarding my two previous books when I visited the USA in 1988.[1]

Rucigay, whose story "The Longest Mission" appears in this book, helped edit the final English version. As an ex-Army Air Forces pilot, John provided the required technical corrections necessary for many of the military and flight terms used. He also transposed all of the stories into a word processor for future editing and helped with the publication of this book in the USA.

Also, special thanks go to Dorothy Rucigay, who helped proofread the English version.

Stephen McFarland's article "Artist Recalls Close WWII Brush," from the July 15, 1983, edition of the *New York Daily News,* appearing in the chapter "A Partisan Sketchbook," is copyright (c) *New York Daily News,* used with permission.

Introduction

This book attempts to document and preserve the accounts of U.S. Army Air Forces personnel who had to land in occupied Yugoslavia and were repatriated to U.S. control zones during World War II. It includes the companion accounts of their Partisan rescuers and, in some cases, follow-up stories of the participants meeting after the war. The stories serve as historical data for future reference, as they are factual accounts of specific events that occurred in those times. The reader must bear in mind, however, that more than 40 years have passed between the actual events and the telling of these stories; naturally, differing versions of the same events occasionally appear in the tales that follow. Also, "Yugoslavia" refers throughout the book to the territorial area that was defined by the World War II borders. With few exceptions, the events described in this volume occurred in Slovenia. Recollections have been slightly edited for clarity and consistency; letters have been reprinted verbatim where possible.

The U.S. military appreciation of the efforts exerted by the Yugoslav Partisans is evident in the following from Captain James Goodwin, head of the Anglo-American Military Mission to Headquarters of the National Army of Liberation and the Partisan Detachments in July 1944:

> As Senior Anglo-American Liaison to Headquarters Slovenia I take this opportunity to thank the National Army of Liberation and the Partisan Detachments of Slovenia and the Slovene people who support the Partisan movement under the leadership of Marshal Tito, for their considerate attention, their kind treatment, and their faithfulness to the Allied cause in the transporting, feeding, housing and the nursing of wounded American fliers who have

been shot-down from the air by the German aggressor. I realize and fully appreciate the sacrifices that are made by you to give our American fliers the kind attention that they have received.

I have heard false rumors, originated by German propaganda, that American fliers have been disfigured and mistreated by Partisan Slovenes. This is not true. I have talked with every American flier that has touched Slovene soil during my time of office here and each man informed me that he received only the kindest treatment and the best care from Partisan Slovenes.

The fliers think that you are wonderful people and they are very proud to be here with you during your struggle for freedom. I assure you that every Allied airplane that you see flying overhead is aware of your noble fight for freedom against the German invader and that each man sincerely hopes that if he is unfortunate enough to be shot down, that he will come into Partisan hands.

In addition, this message from Major General Nathan F. Twining, Commander in Chief of the 15th Air Force, appeared in the February 12, 1945, issue of *Pobeda*, the British monthly for Yugoslavia:

Fourteen months ago the American Air Force started flights across Yugoslavia and many American airmen made a forced landing or bailed out into your country.

Today instead of being German prisoners of war, they are free fighters, owing to the friendly attitude and bravery of men and women of Yugoslavia.

Disregarding your own lives and the security of your families, you saved hundreds of lives of our airmen giving them food, medical aid and shelter. You walked for miles over difficult terrain, across rivers, mountains, through rain and mud, but you always brought out airmen to a safe place.

As the Commander-in-chief of the 15th AAF and in the name of the fathers and mothers of my airmen I am expressing the gratefulness of America for your valiant deeds. Our deepest thanks go also to those who buried our dead and sent me their personal belongings.

Your bravery, patriots, who have acted under serious dangers regardless of your own security, has won the hearts of our airmen for you and has created respect for yourselves and your country.

The High Command of the AAF
February 7, 1945 (UNN)

Chapter 1

A Partisan Sketchbook

It was February 24, 1944. The day was so beautiful in its glorious winter sun that it could truly be called a wonderful creation of God. Although the temperature at night fell below the freezing point, the sun's rays were of sufficient strength to start melting the snow. The highlands had over three feet of snow on the surface, and while the ground cover remained deep in the shady areas, the first flowering buds started to pop out of their wintering shelters on the exposed slopes. The landscape resembled a winter fairy tale. No wonder that one of the greatest Slovene artists, the impressionist Ivan Grohar, chose this particular tract of land for his most impressive and subtle paintings.

The local inhabitants were scattered about the countryside in their small homesteads and were remote from any towns or villages. They had too many worries on their minds to admire the creations of nature. The ongoing war made for the worst of times that had ever befallen them. Mostly women, children, and helpless old men lived on the secluded farms, some of which already lay in ruins. They all had something in common: their concern for the current events and how to survive to live another day. There was scarcely a household in the area that wasn't mourning persons missing or dead.

Most of the men from the scattered hamlets had joined Partisan units, and some were taken to infamous Nazi concentration camps. Unfortunately, there were also a few who collaborated with the occupying forces, and, sad to say, they were even worse than the Germans.

The Partisans were successful from time to time in liberating pockets of territory in the rural areas. On the other hand, the Nazis fortified themselves in the towns and villages. With their numerically superior forces, they occasionally ventured into the liberated areas, setting homesteads on fire and leaving destruction and despair behind them.

At the time of the following event, the Nazi occupation was entering the third year, and despite the Gestapo terror, the resistance to the occupation was spreading all over Slovenia. The local inhabitants were not helpless and did not feel forsaken. They had a well-organized secret service in which nearly everyone participated. Consequently, the Partisans received timely information concerning the enemy's movements and intentions.

Camouflaged guerrilla detachments were scattered deep underground throughout the region. One of the largest in operation in the territory was the *Gorenjska odred* (Northwestern detachment), whose members were capable of enduring the physical hardships and who knew every brook, path, and optimum hiding place where they could find shelter if needed deep in the woods. In one of the detachments was a trio of young, strong, battle-tried scouts — Tomo Bertoncelj, Slavc Zbontar, and Janez Klinar — whose task was to secure the main arterial roadway connecting the Gorenjska and Primorsko roads that also continued into Italy. They were concealed just above the roadway, waiting in ambush for any sudden enemy attack.

At first it did not appear that anything special would occur on that particular, gorgeous morning. But suddenly the stillness was broken by the screaming sounds of German fighter aircraft as they buzzed overhead. They came like a bat out of hell, turned around, and vanished as quickly as they had appeared. The trio agreed that the Germans were up to something. This was verified a minute later when a distant rumbling increased in intensity as the first wave of Allied four-engined bombers flew overhead. The Partisans' hearts leaped with joy at the sight of those aluminum and steel birds high up in the sky, for this was the initial announcement of the long-sought liberty that they all anticipated would arrive soon. But they were also worried that the German fighters would attack the Allied bombers.

Their misgivings were soon justified as they watched two Messerschmitts approach the formation from the direction of the Soriška mountain. The Germans initiated the attack from below the bomber formation before climbing vertically and attacking the rear elements. The victim they chose was a bomber that lagged behind the others. As they closed in and attempted to concentrate their firepower on the vulnerable bomber, they were in turn driven off by the bomber's own machine-gun fire. The elusive and mobile Germans quickly disengaged and vanished as rapidly as they had appeared.

Meanwhile, the three young scouts observing all of the action from the ground could tell from the black smoke that one of the German fighters had been hit. (They later learned from others in the area that the German aircraft had crashed into the massive Porezen mountain.) Unfortunately, they also observed that one of the B-24 Liberators was also trailing black smoke and losing altitude rapidly. It crashed into Ratitovec mountain, where it broke into three main sections that immediately started to burn.

It was a moment during which life in the woods and nearby hamlets seemed to stand still. The local population who had been watching the mighty airplane moments before seemed transfixed; the deer disappeared in the density of the woods and the birds stopped singing.

The trio's attention was not directed to the wrecked airplane but to the parachutists scattered across the blue sky and about to land all over the area. It was the first jump for most of the airmen, and they were not skilled sufficiently to control their direction. Instead of steering to more logical sites such as large grassy clearings, they drifted toward the forest and landed in the tops of trees where most were kept hanging, and some even got hurt. In particular, the Partisans felt sorry for a parachutist who was descending toward a German outpost in Sorica. Of course the man didn't know that since he was unfamiliar with the territory and was kept busy controlling his parachute.

Fortunately, two of the crew members — George Stricker and Corbin McPherson, the nose gunner — were drifting toward the liberated territory between Zali Log and Davce. Stricker bruised himself slightly as he touched down, and McPherson landed so awkwardly that, while swinging to and fro in the top of a tree, he tore his chute and fell to the ground. Luckily, he landed in deep snow and avoided serious injury, just spraining his ankle.

The threesome in hiding did not hesitate to leave their post, rushing forward to aid the parachutists. They did not appear to be far away, but there were hills, valleys, and ravines between them; running in the deep snow did not make it any easier. They were also convinced that the enemy in Sorica had similar intentions.

Luck was with the airmen as the Partisans were quicker than the Germans. The Americans and Slovenians gathered at the foot of the Ratitovec mountain, from where the Partisans escorted the airmen to the mountain hamlet of Martinj Vrh.

And what are the recollections now of the participants of these events? I learned that in 1988, the leader of the Partisan patrol, Janez Klinar (Partisan name: "Gorski"), had retired as an officer and lived in Ljubljana, Slovenia. I tried to contact him on numerous occasions but doubted that he was the person I was seeking until I finally spoke with him. When I first visited and explained why I wanted to talk to him, he seemed surprised that anyone would take any interest in the event. Soon after, he emerged from an adjoining room and laid an American sergeant's chevron on the table in front of me accompanied by a one-dollar bill on which the signature "Sgt. Corbin McPherson" was plainly written.

I asked him how he came across the two objects, and his story follows.

* * * * *

After we watched the tragedy of the American bomber in the air, our first concern was to rescue the airmen and help them in case they were wounded or otherwise in need of help. I knew the terrain where they landed, and as soon as I saw fresh traces in the snow-covered ravine leading to the forest, we scattered to comb the entire area. We stopped several times to catch our breath and to listen for any strange sounds that would draw our attention to anything unusual, but all we heard were the birds singing. However, the trace in the snow was a positive sign; we felt that we were on the right track. This was proven correct shortly afterwards. We saw two unusually clad men at the same time that they spotted us. They were excited and seemed rather indecisive. I was armed and was positive that I knew who the men were, whereas the strangers standing in front of me didn't know if I was their friend or enemy. As I stepped forward, they seemed to be very tense until they caught sight of the small red star on my cap. Then their faces lit up with huge smiles. Since we couldn't communicate in any other way, we kept repeating the words, "Tito, American, Partisan, Stalin, Roosevelt, Churchill." These were the words that Allies and we Partisans used whenever we came across one another.

Shortly afterward, we realized that it was not the time to celebrate. We had to leave the place as soon as possible since we knew that the Germans were also zealous and would not stop searching for the Americans so easily. We picked up their parachutes, folded them, and took them with us since they were valued by the women. Having left the forest we went downhill toward the valley, then crossed the road and the Selščica River. The dark-haired one with the mustache, George Stricker, managed to walk by himself, but the fair-haired Corbin McPherson had problems. We took turns supporting him while we proceeded to vacate the area as rapidly as possible. Later, we stopped for a snack. We did not attempt any conversation then, and that might have caused some mistrust on their part, for we could not tell them where we were taking them or what lay in store for them.

It was already dark when we escorted the airmen into a homestead in Martinj Vrh, where we were received with hospitality. After supper, the Americans produced silken maps to check where they were and how far it was to their base across the Adriatic.

Stricker stretched on a bench alongside the large stove while McPherson sat on the stove after putting on some more clothes. He was shivering from a fever resulting from the sprained ankle. After the gas light was extinguished, the only sound outside was the barking of a chained dog excited by the presence of strangers in the house.

The next day McPherson's health worsened, and we were concerned, since our plan was to reach the peak of Martinj as soon as possible.

News of the Americans staying at Posečnik's spread to the remotest area, and curious neighbors dropped by to see the airmen as if they were some creatures from outer space. One of them, an elderly man who had worked in America, could at least talk a bit with the airmen. Another visitor was the dressmaker Janova Mici, who was happy to receive the nylon parachutes, which she sewed into shirts, blouses, and underwear.

After ten days, McPherson was sufficiently recovered so that the airmen could continue their long journey to Bosnia. Before we left, one of the happy Americans gave me these two objects in remembrance of the occasion.

* * * * *

It so happened that a 17-year-old boy named France Slana was staying at the Presečnik homestead. He originally came from Maribor and had joined the Partisans as a courier for the Gorenjska detachment. Even as a child he had a talent for drawing, so it was no wonder that he carried sketch paper and pencils along with his pistol and hand grenades in his courier bag. It was not uncommon during his daily rest periods to draw a portrait of an acquaintance or his comrade. Naturally, the two Americans provided an immediate alternative; the young artist made drawings of McPherson and Stricker during the two days that the Americans were there. Consequently, Slana carried their portraits in his bag throughout the war and the occupation until peace was achieved.

The Partisan network smuggled McPherson and two of his crew mates to the far southern border of Yugoslavia in a 64-day trek. The Americans flew to Bari, Italy, from a secret airstrip near the Albanian border.

Both McPherson and Slana soldiered to the end of the war. McPherson returned to Texas, and Slana realized his dreams of attending the Academy of Figurative Arts in Ljubljana, Yugoslavia, and becoming an artist. He worked as an illustrator for numerous newspapers, wrote books, and had exhibitions at home as well as across Europe. He became one of the most highly regarded artists in Slovenia and Yugoslavia. After displaying his paintings in numerous art galleries in Europe, Africa, and Asia, he finally entered his first American showing at Automation House in New York under the sponsorship of the 3M Corporation.

To France Slana's surprise, the show's organizer, with the help of Slana's friend Iztok Bartolj, succeeded in tracing Corbin McPherson at his home in Dallas, Texas, and bringing him to New York to attend the exhibition. It was the first meeting between the two former comrades-in-arms since 1944. The well-known *New York Daily News* published an article by Stephen McFarland on July 15, 1983, entitled "Artist Recalls Close WW II Brush":

. . . Even by wartime standards the relationship between France

Corbin McPherson, June 9, 1989, with 1944 picture sketched by France Slana.

Slana and Corbin McPherson was fleeting, but each had his reasons to remember the other.

In 1944, McPherson, of Gainesville, Texas, was a sergeant in the Army Air Corps flying as a nose gunner in a B-24 Liberator out of Bari, Italy, against military and industrial targets in Germany.

On the night of February 26, McPherson's Liberator, en route to bomb ball-bearing factories in Regensburg, Bavaria, was attacked by German fighters. Rocket fire started a blaze in the plane that killed six of the 10 crew members. McPherson and three others bailed out of the burning plane over enemy-occupied Yugoslavia.

McPherson was picked up and hidden from the Germans by a band of Partisans, one of whom was young Slana. "I was one scared Texan," McPherson reminisced yesterday. "But they got me good and drunk, and that satisfied them that I was a real American and not a German spy."

. . . Slana had to return home the next day, but McPherson, then 61 and retired from the Southwest Bell Telephone Co., said he planned to return to Yugoslavia next April, to revisit the place where the Partisans saved his life and spend some time with his old comrades-in-arms.

"I never expected to see him again," said Slana, now 57. "Can

Sketch of George Stricker
made by France Slana,
March 2, 1944.

George R. Stricker, Jr
1st Lt. U.S.A.A.F.
Pilot - B-24 - "Liberator"

France
2-III-1944

you imagine that we found the guy? There were so many ways to
die during the war, but we're both still alive."

The meeting was a unique experience for both of them, but one more person
was missing — George Stricker, whose destiny was also linked to Slana
during the war.

Corbin McPherson not only located George Stricker but also told him about
Slana's sketch of George and that it was in the Yugoslav War Museum in
Ljubljana. George immediately made plans to meet Slana once again.

In June 1988, George Stricker and his wife visited Slovenia to see once more
the places where he, as George says, "was born again." On arriving in
Ljubljana, they visited the Tourist Information Center, which arranged the
first meeting between George and France Slana in 44 years. On that occasion
he also met some persons with whom he had become acquainted during the
war.

Sketch of George Stricker
made by France Slana,
June 9, 1988.

Stricker and his wife wanted to visit the places where George had been. He wanted to meet and thank the hospitable people who had helped him survive the war.

The Ljubljana TV team accompanied him during portions of his trip, resulting in Stricker and his friends being presented on public TV in one of the most popular programs, "Time That Lives." Slovene and Yugoslav TV watchers were able to follow a half-hour broadcast of Stricker's return after 44 years. George related his 1944 experience:

> "While trying to get out of the aircraft, I got sick halfway and did not jump. Part of the plane was in flames, and there was so much smoke that the fumes nearly suffocated me. Even worse, an Me-109 was shooting at me! I finally succeeded in getting loose and bailed out with my parachute. After I landed I saw one of the parachutists hanging from a tree. Another had already been rescued and taken away, and I was relieved to see the star on the approaching Partisan's cap. Our destination was Martin's peak, but

we were not fit enough to reach it before darkness fell.

My fellow crewman who had been rescued earlier was taken to a farmhouse and was uncertain who his hosts were. He wanted to leave, but the Partisans were determined to keep him inside the house. One of them pointed his gun at the airman, who quickly raised his hands and said, "Don't shoot, don't shoot!" But when he saw the red star as the Partisan put on his cap, he was relieved, and a broad smile spread across his face. It was only then that he realized that he was among friends.

It was also interesting how he described Slana's sketches:

When Slana first tried to portray me, his drawing was not especially good, so we all laughed. The second time he tried was much better. It was then that I realized that Slana was a talented person and that he could become an excellent artist if he studied properly. This sketch is invaluable to me because it reminds me of the kind and hospitable people who were willing to help me in time of need. Landing in Partisan territory where I found real friends is the best gift that fate had prepared for me.

George Stricker finished his story by adding how happy he was to be in Slovenia again with his family. Although there were many questions on both sides, several remained unanswered, for some of the persons involved had since died.

A few months later, Corbin McPherson, aged 68 and known as Ben to his friends, decided to visit Yugoslavia. Ben was a sick man suffering from a heart condition, and his doctor warned him against the flight. But his wish was stronger than the risk, and he arrived in Slovenia at the end of May 1989. He came with his brother, Clinton, and his sister-in-law, Clara, both of whom were academic professors in Texas. Ben showed me his cigarette case that had been presented to him by a Partisan. On it was engraved, "To my friend and comrade McPherson — Velimir Svoboda, 27 February 1944." He also had a photograph of a girl with the signature "Štefka"; the date was the same. Ben related the incident and why it was important that he revisit the places he had stayed as a young airman.

* * * * *

On that day that I flew from Italy as a member of the 451st Bombardment Group of the 15th Air Force, I was part of a ten-man crew in a B-24 bomber flying to Regensburg with the intention of destroying the Messerschmitt factories. It was my ninth flight over enemy territory. Before reaching the Alps, some German fighters attacked us and shot down our airplane, killing six of my buddies. I was lucky to be able to bail out, and that was the first time in my life that I had used a parachute. Inexperienced as I was, I descended toward an unknown, hostile, snow-covered land and came down into waist-deep snow on the brim of a precipice. I got rid of my parachute and my jacket, which I later regretted having taken off as I became terribly cold. My fellow crew members obviously landed far away from me, as I did not see a living soul. I used my compass and kept to the rules I was given back at the air base: In case of landing in unknown territory, keep to the south where you might come across the friendly guerrillas and not to the north where you could expect the enemy.

I walked with much difficulty in the deep snow. Besides, it was getting colder and colder. Toward evening I noticed a secluded barn. I pulled myself in and covered myself with leaves. I did not get much sleep since I was apprehensive as to my destiny. After I left the barn the next day I met three women who showed me the way to a house. An elderly man who spoke some English lived there. He told me that he had worked in a mine in Colorado in the States. He succeeded in explaining to me where I was and the situation. Then I followed a ten-year-old boy, who brought me to the Partisans on top of the hill. At first I was told to raise my arms, but after it was clarified who I was, we embraced. I was relieved when I saw another of our crew members, George Stricker.

The Partisans took us to a large farmhouse on top of the hill, where we first warmed up a little around a large stove. We stayed at that farmhouse for several days. The house was frequented by both Partisans and civilians. Everybody kept watching us as if we would perform some miracles. One of the visitors was a young Partisan who made a portrait of me. Another gave me his cigarette case. It was also the place where I encountered this beautiful girl, a Partisan with long hair. She gave me her picture.

* * * * *

There appeared to be sufficient information that would permit us to solve the mystery of the cigarette case and the photograph of the Partisan girl without too much difficulty. However, since we only had three days before Ben's return flight to America, I called Janez Klinar and asked him to help us trace the girl. I was convinced that he was the right person to help us as he still had the American chevron and the one-dollar bill that was signed by Corbin McPherson.

The following day was very lively in Ljubljana's Tivoli Park across from the Museum of the Revolution. It was Youth Day, May 25, and students roamed all

Štefka Puh-Slanina and Corbin McPherson, May 1989, 45 years after their first meeting.

over the wooded areas. We met Matija Žgajnar, the curator of the museum, who had a special surprise for the guests: original drawings by France Slana that he had made over 45 years before. Janez Klinar also appeared and showed Ben the dollar bill with his signature. And Štefka, the girl with the long hair, was there. At first, Štefka and Ben looked at each other for a long time, then they embraced with tears in their eyes. The surrounding crowd soon realized what that moment meant for them.

Could Ben's heart endure all of these surprises? He told us that he was feeling well and suggested that we visit Martinj Vrh, where his story had actually started.

The next day on our way to Martinj Vrh, we stopped for a while at Skofja Loka at the Veterans Union, where we were cordially received. It was there that we learned that Ben would not be able to meet the Partisan who had given him his cigarette case — he had died some years ago.

We drove along the wonderful Šelska valley. The guests were enthusiastic about everything and were interested in every detail. They took a great interest in the farms high up in the hills with churches built on top of the beautiful knolls, such as Plečnik's chapel, which was located in a birch grove in Dolenjska Vas.

We climbed a steep hill after driving through the picturesque old town of Železniki. Ben tensely watched the landscape. He didn't talk much but thought that everything seemed so familiar. Then the cars stopped in front of

McPherson (with cap in center) and friends in Zali Log.

Posečnik's farmhouse in Martinj Vrh. We didn't have to worry about Ben's state of health as he walked toward the brim of the meadow from where there was a wonderful view of the mountain Ratitovec and the hamlets at its base. He stood there, almost motionless, for a long time, looking at the sunlit landscape and obviously reliving the events from his distant past. Shortly he was surrounded by Janez Klinar, France Slana, Matija Žgajnar, and the first commander of the Prešernova Brigade, Igor Javor. Igor was also an airman. Interpreter Vitka Kolar was the busiest person at that moment because there were a lot of questions and answers to be explained. Katarina Posečnik, the landlady of the farmhouse, joined us and invited those present into her house. As Ben crossed the threshold, he stopped when he caught sight of the stove. It was new but similar to the one that he remembered and on which he had slept for some days. Then he climbed up on the stove so that his brother could take a snapshot. Clinton confessed that he had never seen anything like that in his life.

After everyone sat down around the stove, Katarina Posečnik brought in some home-brewed brandy. The guests from Texas claimed it was the best "whiskey" that they had ever tasted. Homemade salami and minced lard were other surprises offered to them. Ben and Štefka sat together and reminisced about their first meeting and the events that had taken place.

During the war, the household had offered food to both Partisans and Americans: a large bowl of *ričet,* barley boiled with beans. In it were some black dots that Ben did not like. He decided to taste the *ričet* only after Štefka removed them. He had liked that beautiful girl, perhaps the only bright light in that unknown and uncertain environment. He had then taken a large silver ring with "B-24" engraved on it from his finger and handed it to her. Štefka put the ring on her finger, and it pleased her. As she had nothing to give him in return, she gave him her photograph.

That first meeting, which had lasted only a little over an hour, was something that they had never forgotten. When we parted at the railway station in Ljubljana, Ben assured us that he was feeling well. After all, he did return to visit the place where he was "reborn" 45 years before and was very elated.

And what was the fate of the rest of the crew from the aircraft named *Wee Willie?* One, Lloyd Cook, was captured by the Germans. The other, James Boornazian, was among the last to bail out, landing in the top of a tall fir tree above Novaki village near Cerkno in the vicinity of the Yugoslav-Italian border. Not far from his landing site were two strong Partisan Brigades, the Prešernova and the Vojkova. Individuals from these units were the first persons to arrive, helping James to climb down from the tree. Since he was bruised from the descent, he was taken to the farmer Tratnik, who treated his wounds. He was then escorted to a neighbor's house, which served as the Prešernova Brigade's propaganda center. The Partisan artist in residence at the

Sketch of crew member
James Boornazian
made by Dore Klemen-
čič, May 1944.

time was Dore Klemenčič ("Maj"), who was responsible for illustrations in
the illegal Partisan daily paper. The February 28, 1944, issue of the paper
included a drawing of air combat between German and American airplanes as
well as a portrait of James Boornazian. From "Allied Airmen and Prisoners of
War Rescued by the Slovene Partisans," it was evident that he returned safely
to America. His portrait is on display in the Ljubljana Museum.

Chapter 2

Ive Šubic and
the American Airmen

During March 1944, six American airmen — Aron Sosnin, James O'Camp, Robert W. Glasby, William Benton, Charles Grant, and Roswell Casada — the oldest 25 at the most, found themselves in the skies above the impenetrable forests of Kocevski Rog in southern Slovenia. Their bomber had been separated from the rest of the bomber formation and attacked by the enemy while returning from a mission over Austria. They were hit by German fighters based at the Cerklje airport near Brezice.

The Americans bailed out, their parachutes scattered all over the sky, with most landing in the leafless trees. Fortunately, they were in the Rog forests — the enemy seldom searched the uninhabited dark and quiet beech and pine forests that had been a wilderness for centuries. Inhabitants of the sparsely populated settlements lived in peaceful coexistence with the wild animals. It was no accident that the Partisans had chosen these wooded areas for their base operations, hospital, and printing shop.

Near one of the local sites close to Pugled, named King's Stone by the natives, was the location of Slovene Partisan post TV 14 with its print shop. In the art department working as an illustrator was a 19-year-old lad from Gorenjska, in the northwestern part of Slovenia. Since painting had been his hobby before the war, he became extremely useful to the print shop. At night he and some of the other boys worked on Partisan propaganda material such as brochures and newspapers, leaflets, and the like, but in the daytime he worked with a pickax, shovel, or saw to help build barracks. Although that was the main contribution of Ive Šubic over 45 years ago, he later became a well-known painter and sculptor.

In the days of his youth, Ive and the rest of the boys and girls had no connection with the outside world. Consequently, every unusual event was interesting and welcomed. Every time they heard the rumbling of hundreds of heavy bombers above them, they stopped working and watched, from the first appearance in the sky until the far-off dots disappeared completely from the horizon. This became the daily routine from the late winter of 1944 on.

March 19 started out the same. Ive Šubic and the underground print shop courier Janez were ready to leave the Urška print works for a two-hour walk to Doljna Briga. They adjusted their ski boots to the skis and set out in fine weather toward their destination. On the way they stopped at an old house and hid their skis. They carefully swept away any telltale tracks that might attract the enemy and continued on their way.

They returned along the same route after they had finished their business. To their surprise they found that the skis were missing (later discovering that they had been taken by some other Partisans). There was nothing left to do but continue wading through the very deep snow toward Rog. It was noon and lunchtime before they finally emerged, tired from the hike, at the edge of a sunlit clearing about a hundred meters square. Simultaneously, on the other side of the clearing, they perceived two figures slowly moving toward them. They wondered who on earth they could be as there were no houses, courier routes, or camouflaged posts anywhere near their present location. As the distance was too great to confirm if the silhouettes were the enemy, Ive and Janez grabbed their automatic rifles and prepared themselves for the worst. They couldn't use any of the terrain for protection as the ground was flat. Therefore, with guns pointed straight ahead, they advanced toward the strangers. More details became discernible as they got closer. They also noticed that the strangers were holding Colts pointed at them.

The uncertainty of the next move by either side was unbearable. Even the slightest, most innocent gesture could have been fatal. But it was soon clear to the two Partisans that these men were not Germans. Neither, from the appearance of their clothes, were they Partisans. So who were they?

The riddle was soon solved after taking a few more hesitant steps forward. Ive first noticed the long scarf that the closest one wore around his neck. Then he noticed an insignia that fliers usually wore on their uniforms. Well, they must be Allied airmen, thought Ive as he lowered his arms. But the two strangers remained extremely cautious.

Ive wore a pair of nice black trousers, cleaned and beautifully pressed. He wasn't wearing his cap; it was stuck in his belt and unnoticed by the strangers.

They all wondered at the next step, since up to then no word had been spoken. Then Ive thought of his cap with the red star on it and, holding it so that the star was in plain sight, stated: "Partisan, Partisan, Tito." Obviously, these were the correct words, for a look of relief crossed the strangers' faces immediately. Any further discussion was unnecessary, as the four young men

Ive Šubic sketch of his encounter with the American airmen in 1944.

shook hands and embraced one another in the middle of the sunlit, snowy clearing.

Only then did Ive notice that the shorter, fair-haired airman had a wound in his neck. Although he had stopped bleeding, it was evident that he had lost much blood, since he moved with great difficulty. The other one, with a dark complexion, was a giant.

They still had a long way to go before they reached the courier station. The three of them had to continuously help the wounded airman, who was completely exhausted. A mule had been harnessed to a sled loaded to the top with Partisan literature and had been waiting for them. In spite of the fact that there was hardly any room left to transport a man, the American was placed on top. Unfortunately, it didn't take too long before the sled broke apart. At that point, the wounded man was placed on the mule. The scene was so comical to his dark-complexioned companion that he constantly made jokes about the fact, laughing and staying in good humor for the rest of the trip.

The unusual caravan reached courier post TV 14 at dusk. They snacked and took leave of one another. The wounded American thanked Ive, and in remembrance of the encounter in the Rog forest presented Ive with his scarf, which Ive kept until his death in 1989. A few hours later the wounded man was under the care of doctors while Ive continued on his way to Urska for night duty.

Thinking back and reliving the encounter that took place 45 years ago had been a positive memory for Ive. He was aware that he had done a good job contributing to the Allied cause, especially for the Americans who were eventually reunited with their families. The entire episode was successfully concluded because both sides restrained themselves from intuitively pulling the trigger before establishing positive identification. The split-second hesitation prevented a dreadful ending to this story.

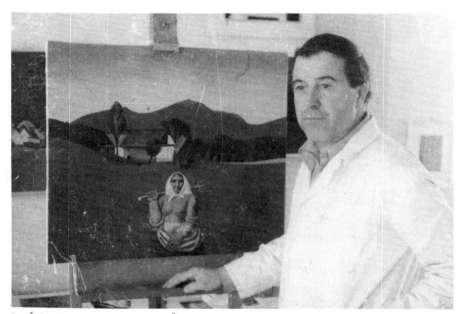

Ive Šubic the artist in his studio in Škofja Loka.

Chapter 3

Airmen in the
Snow-Covered Alps

"There is no telling as to what a person will do to get back to where he belongs. Yesterday was my day. I was surprised it wasn't anything like I thought. If I'm lucky, I'm now on my way home. I wish I could find some of the fellows."

This note was written by Sergeant Ascencion Gonzales from Tulsa, Oklahoma, to Janko Novak ("Zdravko") in Slovenia. When I visited Janko many years after the war, he showed me the piece of paper that he kept as a reminder of the most terrible and exciting night that he and two of his comrades had ever spent in their lives. The yellowed paper showed the effects of time, but the subject matter never lost its value. How could Zdravko forget the hours and hours spent under the most difficult conditions trying to reach the American airmen that were forced to bail out after their B-17 Flying Fortress from the 96th Bombardment Squadron, 2nd Bomb Group, had been shot down near Klagenfurt, Austria, on March 19, 1944? Accompanied by Mirko Faganel ("Čevada") and Kristelj Erbežnik ("Ciril"), they pushed through the deep snow to save an unknown man's life. (Faganel perished a few months later in a battle with the Germans; Erbežnik died after the war.)

Zdravko placed additional documents on the table that provided details of the method used to reach the airmen and included the names of two additional members of the same crew that were also rescued: Thomas W. Farbes from North Carolina and Russell W. Phillips from Jeffersonville, Indiana. I asked him to relate his experience of the event.

* * * * *

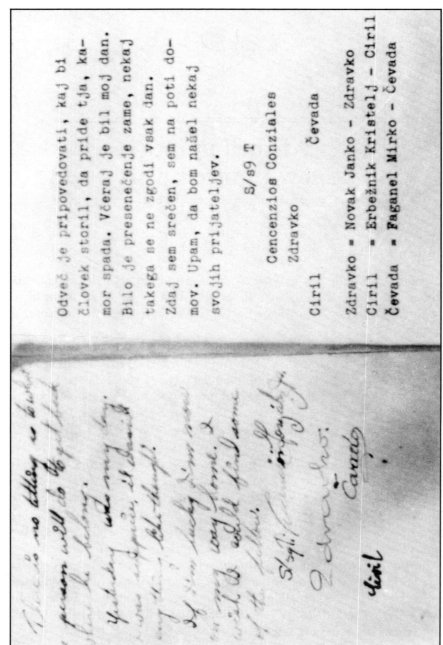

The note written by Ascencion Gonzales with a Slovene translation next to it.

The heavy rainfall during the early part of March 18 turned into a blizzard. By nightfall more than a half-meter of new snow had fallen, bending branches of trees and bushes down to the ground. It had stopped snowing by the time it got dark. The skies had cleared, and the combined effect of all of the stars reflecting off of the new snow produced a daylight effect. A fox barked somewhere near our camp, probably because he could not hunt that night due to the brightness and the snowfall.

The following day, March 19 (St. Joseph's day), we were awakened by gorgeous, sunny weather. Since I was on duty that day, I was the first to arise as there was additional work that I had to complete. As we had to exercise precaution, we made the usual inspection around the campsite. I noticed some fresh tracks in the snow that I knew by previous agreement had been made by a nearby farmer. He would take his horses across the trails that we normally used in order to trick any Germans who might be tracking us. Since it was a holiday, we planned to meet several of our comrades from Javornik and Bela.

By the time I came back, breakfast — consisting of herbal tea and *mesta*, a cooked potato and flour mixture known only in the northwestern part of Slovenia — was ready. As the couriers departed, I left the camp for a large rock from which I could view the entire valley below our post. Only a few days remained before the arrival of spring. I reflected on how the past winter might be the last spent in the woods, a thought in the minds of many Partisans who longed for peace and freedom. We would soon be free; no more ambushes or snow. Yes, the snow. I could not imagine then that I would still be fed up with snow to this day!

My daydreaming was interrupted by a distant but clearly audible rumbling. It suddenly dawned on me: They are coming! A few moments later, numerous groups of aircraft appeared high overhead, steadily approaching the border between Yugoslavia and Austria. We sensed that their destination was not too far north of us. The planes glistened like silver birds in the air. Shortly after they flew over the Alps, we heard the sounds of the enemy antiaircraft artillery. After bombing their targets, the planes passed over intermittently on their return.

Our attention was drawn to a single plane nearing our position. Its rumbling noise sounded like a wounded wild animal. We guessed that it was hit, which was confirmed by the trail of smoke. Almost simultaneously, we noticed the small dots separating from the aircraft turn into small objects suspended from parachutes. Shortly thereafter, the plane exploded and split in two — half falling on Mount Golica and the other half below Mount Stol. We watched five of the parachutists as they descended, growing larger and larger. One drifted toward Golica and another must have landed in the mountains on the Austrian side while two drifted even farther toward the valley. However, we were very excited while following the descent of the fifth one, who we saw land on top of

Janko Novak ("Zdravko"), early 1944.

Janko Novak 40 years later.

Mount Belščica.

Without the slightest hesitation I said, "Who is going to go with me to rescue the parachutist?"

"I am," replied courier Čevada, a strong young fellow from Ozeljan near Novo Gorica. After a short discussion on the merits for including a third person in our search party, we were joined by Ciril from Javornik.

We walked cautiously in the path beaten in the snow, wondering about the health and state of mind of the parachutist. Who is he and where did he come from? we wondered. Would we reach him first, or would the Germans or even the collaborators?

No. We had to reach him first, at any cost! We hurried, as every minute was precious. But we had to stop suddenly as we rushed along the path, because the track made by Nočev Jože's horse ended.

We had difficulty pulling our legs out of the meter-deep snow as we struggled up the hill. It was as if we had fallen into clay pits. We then realized the enormity of the task we had undertaken, since we were only at the foothill of the mountain. "We should have snowshoes," stated Ciril.

"Yes, and many other things, too," I added. In single file, we alternated being first in the deep, wet snow. We proceeded slowly, encouraging each other. Occasionally one of us would tell a joke, which was soon followed by a curse when one of us would sink deeper into the snow-covered juniper. We climbed straight up for fear of causing an avalanche if we traversed the slope.

As we approached the mountain plateau, the snow-covered pine trees glittered like silver in the afternoon sun shining on the Julian Alps. Had we really been walking so long? We had to hurry up. We were all in a sweat and our clothes stuck to our body. We were wet up to our waists as if we had waded through a river. We continued to struggle until we finally reached the plateau.

The wind swept over the plateau. What a change! It was a little easier to walk as the snow was encrusted with ice. Then our clothes started to ice up, and a biting cold wind penetrated to our bones. When we reached the mountain shacks, only their slanting roofs jutted through the snow. We did not rest but continued on our way toward the summit, accompanied by the wind. At first it sounded like a baby's whimpering from afar but slowly turned into a more distinct, angry sound. It gained in crescendo until it reached full power and sounded like a pack of starving wolves.

This continued intermittently. As the force of the wind diminished, the sound level decreased. However, when it was almost exhausted, it would start to increase once more. This wind-song refrain accompanied us, making our hike more terrible and awesome.

The airman must be somewhere in this area! We soon caught sight of some footprints in the snow haphazardly going in all directions. Had anyone arrived before us? We thought not, since we found that all of the footprints were identical, seemingly belonging to the chutist. We split up and searched in three separate directions, criss-crossing the earlier footprints for a while until Ciril shouted, "Janko, look; there he is. I can see him. Let's go over there!"

With a few jumps I was beside him. In front of me stood a man of rather short stature, dark complexioned, clad in his one-piece flying suit and felt boots. He stared at me steadily as if he was thinking of something. Soon his brow smoothed and his face brightened. He lifted his arm pointing to my cap with the five-pointed red star on it lit up by the last rays of the setting sun and then, relieved, shouted, "Tito! Tito!"

"Yes, Tito," I answered him, whereupon he embraced me. So, holding one another in our frozen clothes, we stood in the wind on the summit of Belščica on the border, he an American airman thousands of miles from his homeland, and me, a free man and Partisan. We kissed each other as if we were old friends. By that time Ciril and Čevada joined us. He also shook hands with them and embraced them.

Although dead tired just a few moments before, we forgot about that for the present. The task we had set upon was accomplished. Ahead was the return trip.

"Janko, a little brandy would do us good. I would do anything for a drink," Ciril said.

"I would do twice as much just for a sip of tea. I have a frog in my throat," I replied.

Just at that moment the airman took some cigarettes out of his pocket and handed them out. I do not smoke, but the other three lit their cigarettes, inhaling their first puff with special pleasure. Ciril's eyes flashed with extreme enjoyment. We were all silent. I kept watching them smoking, thinking how happy and thankful they were for small gifts. Then we tried to express our thoughts but were unsuccessful. At one point Čevada said something in Italian, and the airman answered in Spanish. Then, as if by a miracle, we started to hold a conversation. He told us that they had been hit by antiaircraft fire over Klagenfurt. The pilot had been mortally wounded in the throat and head. He had remained in the plane, but the others had bailed out just in time. We saw the rest ourselves. He, Ascencion Gonzales, was the flight engineer and had bailed out last. Afterwards he drifted toward the Karavanke Alps.

He then showed us where he had landed — right at the edge of a steep precipice under the rock walls. Another meter or so farther north and he would have been killed in the crags. Our rescue mission would have been in vain. He also showed us how he had dug a deep hole in the surface and wrapped the parachute around himself for protection against the biting north wind. I picked up the parachute, and we set out for the valley. As long as we walked along the plateau we didn't have any special problems. They started only after we entered the area with the pine trees and junipers, where the snow was wet and softer. The airman could hardly walk due to his felt boots with electric wiring. He was constantly sinking, and, with difficulty, we dragged him as well as ourselves out of the deep snow. Nightfall was approaching, so we tried to walk as fast as possible. We eventually came across a plowed trail. After hiking for some time along the trail leading to Rovte, we stopped. I then suggested to the others that they lag behind me a short distance since the Germans had probably followed our progress with binoculars from their post at the power station in Javorniški Rovt. I then proceeded cautiously, aware of the possible presence of the enemy lying in ambush. The collaborators might also be trying to intercept us. Luckily, no one came.

It was nearly pitch dark when we finally arrived at our camp where we were enthusiastically received by our comrades. We were all glad that the rescue concluded with a happy ending. The other members of the underground, the couriers, and our secretary Slovenko had meanwhile returned to our camp. Slovenko had previously been informed about the crashed plane and the airman who had bailed out over Belščica. With the high morale in the camp, he was certain that we would try to find him, even though it was a longshot.

Gonzales sat by the fire drying his clothes and warming his frozen body. The cozy warmth of the place raised the spirits of all of us, especially when the pleasant smell of cooked supper pervaded our nostrils.

After supper, the Jesenice underground personnel took the American with them to Javorniški Rovt. They stopped at Kajženik's, a hospitable Partisan house. Kajženik's father was surprised to have a real American visitor in the house. Others also arrived to have a look at him. While they would have liked to talk to him, the language barrier posed a problem.

Meanwhile, another courier named Stefan and I proceeded to his homestead where we both climbed atop the *kmečka peč*, a high square stove used for sitting or lying and baking. His three sisters offered us food as if it were a holiday. By the time we left and returned to the camp it was dawn. As soon as Gonzales caught sight of me he jumped up and pressed me tightly against his bosom and greeted me, "Tito, Tito!" Although I tried to inform him that my name was Janko, he kept calling me Tito. He stuck to me like a child to his mother.

In a discussion with Čevada, Gonzales stated that what he had just experienced seemed unbelievable. It was at this point that he wrote the few lines mentioned at the beginning of this story.

A surprise awaited us the next day. Couriers brought in two more airmen to the camp above Javorniški Rovt. One had been saved by a Carinthian Partisan, but the other one had just landed on a courier trail.

* * * * *

I had tried to obtain more information about the rescue of the other two airmen from Gonzales's plane. After extensive inquiries, it was Janko Novak — "Zdravko" — who once more provided me with the data.

* * * * *

At that time the Carinthian couriers of the K2 outpost were stationed in Velika Suha. Their bunkered stronghold was built of wooden logs. While they obtained their water from the brook Suha, they also waded through it frequently in order to throw the Germans off-track, especially in the winter when there was deep snow. While the courier team consisted of strong, good-humored young fellows always ready for some jokes, they were also daring and very efficient when necessary.

Two courier routes lead from that stronghold. Very early on the morning after the blizzard, Tine and Jože set out on one of the routes. They knew that because of the fresh snow their walk would take longer and be more difficult. It promised to be a fine day; the moon was fading away and the early sun was glowing red on the horizon. They cursed both the snow and the Germans as they slowly advanced along the trail toward the place where they were supposed to meet their counterparts coming from the opposite direction.

"It seems to me that we will experience something special today," said Tine.

Rescue operations usually occurred during the worst weather conditions.

"Don't be silly. What the deuce could happen to us in such snow? There is no fool around who would climb up here," angrily replied Jože as he struggled through the snow. By the middle of the morning they had reached the summit of Golica where they rested in the hot sun sheltered against the cold wind.

As they snacked they watched the American bombers flying overhead toward the border and heading for Villach and Klagenfurt. After the bombardment, the American planes were attacked by German fighters. As the couriers had an excellent view from atop Golica, they noticed one of the Allied planes was hit and saw the parachutes. It was like watching a movie.

As Tine and Jože continued on the route that overlooked the German positions, their routine included additional tasks that lasted until nightfall. They were dead tired when they returned to their camp and were just about to sit down on their beds made of boards when the door opened and two strangers in uniform entered the stronghold. "Partisans, Tito," they blurted out. We knew immediately that they were the American airmen who had bailed out the day before. They told us that there had been nine of them in the plane, and the two of them were lucky to find themselves close to each other after they had landed. One of them had landed right on the courier trail. They rationalized that the trail might lead them to someone who could assist them.

The airmen were Sergeants Farbes and Phillips. They had waited on the path for two hours, hoping that someone would come by. (The couriers in the bunkers heard the rumbling of the plane but could not see the parachutists as their stronghold was somewhat sheltered by high fir trees.)

Both Americans had wrapped their parachutes around themselves and, half-awake, spent the night in the open. In the morning they had buried their chutes in the snow and set out following the trail. Before long, they saw a group of armed persons with backpacks from a distance. (They were the couriers returning from their various mission tasks.) It was clear to them, seeing their clothes and caps, that they were not the enemy. They could only be Partisans, whom the airmen had heard about at their air base in Italy. However, they did not wish to reveal themselves immediately and cautiously viewed the column's line of direction. They were much surprised when they noticed that when the men with the backpacks reached the end of the trail by the stream, they began wading upstream through the brook. The two airmen followed the same procedure and, after hearing voices, discovered that the new trail leading from the brook led straight to the stronghold.

Farbes and Phillips stayed with the underground personnel and couriers for a few days. They left their flying suits and flight boots in the camp after substitute clothing and shoes were provided. They felt comfortable among the Partisans and at the same time appreciated the discipline and comradeship offered.

They left the camp for their return journey, and, after numerous changes of escorting guides, they finally reached a Partisan airport. They flew to Bari, Italy, on April 16, 1944.

* * * * *

Ludvik Bem ("Slavc") relates the tale of the fourth member of the same crew.

* * * * *

Our post was above Sveče and Rož in Carinthia. When we heard the planes we started to count them but gave up shortly as there were too many. One of the planes left its formation and crashed soon afterward.

We saw some parachutists bail out. Three of them parachuted high up in the Alps, the rest of them in Rož, except for one who approached our post. When it became evident that the airman would land near us, I took my comrade, Dušan Faganel — "Danko" — with me to bring the airman to our post.

Although the Germans arrived at the area, they only fanned out and searched 150 to 200 meters from the landing site. The fact that the airman landed only 50 meters from us probably saved his life.

When Danko and I approached the airman, he was terribly frightened. After all, although I had a cap with a five-pointed red star on it, I was wearing a nominal German uniform. Once again, it was just the star that cleared everything., The airman, as many others before had done, started to shout, "Tito, Tito, Tito," and then he embraced me. Afraid that the Germans might be nearby, I tried desperately to make the American keep quiet. He folded his chute and followed us as we anticipated seeing the Germans at any moment.

Tension slackened after it got dark. Only then did we try to obtain more information from the airman. He told us that he was a tail gunner and that he was from Virginia. He said that they had been told to immediately come in contact with the Partisans if they were shot down. He was a handsome youth of about 22 to 24 years of age and wore a signet ring with a picture of his girlfriend in it. He told us that he would marry her. After he spent the night sleeping we gave him some clothes more suitable for snow and took him to the West Carinthian Headquarters. Franc Primižič ("Marko"), the commander, spoke rather good English. Unfortunately, we arrived after lunch. As the airman was hungry, the commander offered to let him scrape the whole cauldron for whatever food was left. To our amazement, the American borrowed a spoon and scraped everything that remained in the kettle.

At our parting, he promised to parachute a box of chocolates if he ever succeeded in returning safely to his squadron.

* * * * *

Although the B-17 normally carried a crew of ten, the destiny of only four of them was known. Of the remaining crew, the airman that was burned in the plane was found later by the Carinthian Partisans and buried behind Golica. The destiny of those that drifted in the direction of Rož, Sveče, and Bistrica nad Podgorje remained a mystery. After the war we tried to find some traces of the rescued airmen in the United States, but our endeavors were in vain — too much time had passed.

Writer and
journalist
Ladislav
Kiauta.

Chapter 4

The Story of Carl Lannier

The well-known Slovene writer and journalist Ladislav Kiauta related a dramatic meeting with some American airmen during World War II.

* * * * *

It was early spring 1944 in the Sava River valley, and the first signs of vegetation were starting to appear. The slopes of the Bohor mountain were still covered with snow on that day, March 19. In order to reduce the waiting period for the next Partisan courier to appear, we decided on a one-hour walk uphill to intercept him at a remote homestead that was exposed to the morning sun on the top of the open ridge. This mountainous area was half-liberated from the enemy. German troops seldom pursued the local Kozjansko Partisan troops. It was only a month ago that our XIV Division advanced through here across the Kozjansko toward Celje. Now there were many Partisan courier outposts spread throughout Slovenia. Members of the local outpost occasionally hung around the village of Ložice.

That particular day was a holiday. There wasn't a cloud in the early morning dark blue sky. I was with two other very important couriers, Tone and Loški Tine, a farmer from Ložice. We started to plow uphill through the snow, stopping once in a while in the open areas to admire the wonderful view of the Sava valley and the distant landscape defining the broad mountain ridge.

We suddenly became aware of a distant rumbling of aircraft south of us. The first groups of the four-engined bombers soon appeared in their characteristic formations heading north. The Allied air forces would have had a nice day for the trip if they didn't have to face the impending battle with the enemy. Additional groups appeared on the horizon until they literally filled up the sky.

We could not count them as there were hundreds and hundreds of them! Reflected sunlight made them appear to be made of glass. The rumble grew deafening as it echoed everywhere in the valley. We imagined it was not pleasant for the bewildered and frightened Germans sheltered somewhere there. Small fighter aircraft circled, leaving curled contrails in the blue sky. For us it was a beautiful and magnificent scene. For the residents of the Austrian and German towns that were the recipients of the deadly cargo, it would be viewed differently.

The aircraft flew above us for a long time. We could still hear the distant rumbling after we reached the homestead on the mountaintop. "They must be going to Vienna," said the homesteader from the threshold of his house as he welcomed us with outstretched arms. My two companions were quite friendly with him as he was also a courier. There wasn't a single person in these lonely mountain areas who wasn't an active member in the Liberation movement.

We sat down on the bench by the fireplace and, while snacking, talked about subjects that pervaded our lives: progress of the fight against the enemy in our homeland and the world situation on other fronts. The conversation continued for about one hour, and it was close to noon when the householder's daughter rushed in breathlessly and cried, "They are fighting! They are fighting in the sky! Come out and watch!"

There was no need to tell us again — we ran out in no time. Pairs of fighter planes were chasing other aircraft at high speeds, and we had to strain our eyes to distinguish which planes were German and which were Allied. Although the Germans outnumbered the Allied craft, we watched one German plane attacking two American planes from the north. We identified them from their wing markings as we gazed up at them as if we were in an upside-down gallery. The German fighter skillfully encircled his opponents, darting from one side and then the other, diving below and returning again and again. The Allied planes performed likewise and, after a brief separation, pounced on the enemy. In between the whining noises of the engines we would hear the occasional bursts of machine-gun fire. The progress of the dogfight drifted toward the town of Zidani Most when we noticed that one of the planes had been hit and started to fall earthward. We silently hoped that it was a German plane.

The householder and Tone went into the house, but Tine and I continued watching the squadrons of Allied planes returning from their air raid in their usual formation. However, we noticed that one of the last planes in the group was trailing smoke. Soon afterward, we could see flames coming from its tail. But the bomber continued to fly serenely and maintained its place in the formation. We lost sight of it for a few seconds and then noticed as the flight approached us that it started to lag behind the others. As it flew overhead, the nose tilted downward, and after an explosion we saw the right wing come off and fall to the ground as the plane spiraled down toward us. (Later on Tine and I recalled seeing two small black dots next to the plane.) We couldn't watch any longer as we had a maddening fear that the plane might hit us! We broke out in a cold sweat as we could hear the noise of the falling bomber grow louder as it approached us. Where could we hide in that open area? We hesitated for a quarter of a second before we hopelessly flung ourselves into the packed snow and closed our eyes. There was a huge, horrible blast above us, and, as we opened our eyes, we could see that the plane had crashed with some force barely 20 yards from us, slightly below the homestead and into a rift valley that was bordered by trees on the opposite hill. It is strange how time slows down when a person experiences a catastrophe or some other dangerous event. We distinctly remembered how, with a hellish noise, the enormous plane crashed after cutting a swath through the trees, sitting down on its nose like a huge bird. After swinging a few times, it stood still with its burnt tail high in the air, nearly as high as the homestead. Simultaneously, a large smoke-filled flame burst from it as I jumped up.

"Lie down!" screamed Tine as he pulled me down. "What if there are bombs on board?" Luckily, there were none; otherwise the explosion would have swept us as well as the homestead with all of its inhabitants off of the hill.

The householder and Tone rushed out of the house; with disheveled hair and bulging eyes, they looked like madmen. They must have experienced a similar horror standing by the house. After all, the bomber had also been aimed at them! The plane burned more fiercely now. It was quite impossible to approach the bomber, especially since the ammunition was aflame and the sounds of it detonating filled the air.

There were other surprises to come. A parachutist floated past us, as if in a dream. He was drifting sideways in our direction. He was so low above the hill that we could distinguish a man in a green flight suit among the strings. We rushed down the hill to reach him as rapidly as possible before the Germans arrived. Along the path we met the first villagers from Ložice hurrying up to the crash site. Among them were armed Partisan soldiers from the Kozjansko detachment who were camped in a deserted hunting lodge.

Tine was lucky and found the parachutist first. His chute had entangled itself at the top of a spreading fir tree from which he descended by sliding down the rough trunk. When Tine arrived, he found the exhausted airman resting under the tree with his head bent down. When Tine tried to inform the airman that he was in no danger, the man immediately tried to swallow an aspirin-like pill. Tine knocked the pill from the airman's hand, fearing that it was poison being swallowed in despair. As they stood there looking at each other and trying to communicate, additional villagers arrived and attempted a dialogue with the airman in several languages but to no avail, as none of the inhabitants knew English. The black-haired man, not typically American-looking (even though we did not know what a typical American looked like), watched us for a long time. Obviously he still did not know where he was or who we were. We tried to make ourselves understood with words such as "comrade," pointing to ourselves and then repeating the word when we pointed at him. We kept babbling on, telling him that we were Partisans, that we would take care of him and not let him fall into the hands of the Germans, about the war against fascism, Hitler, and so on.

Finally, we mentioned Tito. Having heard the name, he understood us completely. At that moment I saw this combat-experienced airman weep tears of joy. He wanted to embrace all of us in turn with his bleeding hands. He had also hurt his leg when he landed. We lifted and carried him into the village.

Arriving at Loški Tine's house, the villagers brought the airman as much food as they had in addition to some drinks. However, the American wouldn't touch anything. A woman Partisan, Tanja, cut through his heavy, one-piece flight suit to clean and bandage his wounds.

He was not armed. Whatever sweets and chocolates he had with him, he shared among the children. Many of the villagers and local Partisan soldiers and couriers visited with the American. He could tell from their faces that they looked upon him as a friend. He placed his silken map on the table, and we showed him approximately where the plane had crashed. Suddenly he asked, "Where are my comrades?" We hesitated before telling him that five burnt bodies remained in the wreckage. He understood that and buried his face in his hands as he cried.

With the imminent threat of Germans arriving from the nearest larger town, we escorted the rescued airman to the woods above the village where he would sleep overnight on the ground with only tent canvas as insulation. Since the airman was entrusted to me, I tried to keep him warm with my own body throughout the night, but he was shaking and shivering so much that he couldn't sleep. I didn't know if it was due to the shock that he had experienced or because he was not used to sleeping on the bare ground. The next morning the Partisans took him to the hospital where he met a fellow crewman, Carl Lannier, who had been gravely injured when he had bailed out. He was then escorted via courier outposts on a long and painstaking hike across the mountains and rivers, avoiding the Germans en route, before arriving at the Partisan airfield in Bela Krajina in southern Slovenia.

* * * * *

Janez Šiško was a Partisan who had been seriously wounded when a German bullet went through his throat. When he recovered he was not capable of rejoining a combat team, but he was determined to continue helping the Partisans. Therefore, he enrolled in a general course for training as a medical

Male nurse Janez Šiško, who treated badly wounded Carl Lannier for several months.

orderly. Later on, based on the knowledge of medicine that he had learned and due to the shortage of doctors, he joined a hospital to help his wounded comrades. After a particularly fierce battle in Styria during which there were a great number of dead as well as wounded, Janez Šiško was assigned the responsibility of bringing a group of severely wounded Partisans to safety.

Transporting the wounded on stretchers along a virtually impassable ravine in the deep snow while being fired on from above by German snipers was almost a hopeless task. But there was no other choice. After this ordeal, all of the 15 wounded were settled in an abandoned icy pillbox. It was dangerous to light a fire since the Germans in the surrounding area would have noticed the smoke immediately. Life was prolonged for most of the injured in the first

A Partisan hospital deep within the forest where many of the wounded, including Carl Lannier — "Joe" from California — were treated.

hospital of the XIV Division. However, one of the soldiers, Mirko Košir ("Samo"), was dying. The not-yet 18-year-old had not been able to withstand the additional strain of the previous night's march. Another Partisan, Alojz Grča, also died soon after. They were the only two deaths among the 103 wounded who were eventually treated at the hospital. Coincidentally, one of the most badly wounded persons treated at that hospital on March 19 was airman Carl Lannier.

Janez Šiško and Milan Alič ("Matevšek") had first heard the moaning of the seriously injured airman as he lay on a hill opposite the hospital, some 100 yards away. Matevšek immediately set out in the direction of the sounds, which had become barely audible. At first he saw a chute in the tree and a moment later a stranger sitting on the ground red with the blood oozing from a wound in his throat. He also had many bruises covering his body. After Matevšek snatched the chute from the tree and removed all traces that might jeopardize the location of their hospital, the two orderlies carefully carried the airman across the ravine to the hospital.

Janez attended to the wounds. He removed all of the clothing that was torn and tattered. He cleansed the wounds and disinfected all the body bruises. The gunshot wound in the man's throat and the wound in his leg worried him the most. He offered some brandy, which the airman refused. Then he tried chamomile tea, ladling it by teaspoons, but the tea flowed out from the wound in the neck. The wound became festered, and the man's condition went from bad to worse. Another slightly injured airman who had arrived at the hospital was also convinced of his comrade's poor condition. He initially hoped to wait a day or two so that the two of them could travel together, but after observing the plight of the other airman, he was not sure that he would survive.

But Janez Šiško was not of the same opinion. With Matevšek, he walked to the various farms in the region soliciting food for the wounded man. He requested tea as well as an enormous amount of clean bandages. The tea was the airman's only food for weeks.

Coupled with the fresh air, Janez's care eventually paid off, and the wound gradually healed. People at the hospital started to call the airman "Pepi" — possibly because he fell out of the sky on St. Joseph's day (Pepi is a shortened version of Joseph) — or "Pappy," which was easier to pronounce. Since no one at the hospital knew any English, Pappy began to start taking an interest in the Slovene language. He started by learning names of objects. As his health progressed, he improved his communication with the people in the hospital. The wound in his throat finally healed, and he was then able to eat everything. Shortly thereafter he began receiving packages from the members of the Allied mission. He shared everything with the wounded men at the hospital; in addition, he was cheerful and witty. He was always ready to help anyone. To while away the time he listened to the radio and sometimes played cards. In short, Pappy/Carl Lannier from California, a hopeless case whose hours had been numbered only months before, was almost completely recovered just prior to his thirtieth birthday — October 8 — except for his leg.

On September 18, 1944, after seven long months at the hospital, Carl Lannier had to leave. Everyone had gotten attached to him, and they grieved very much at the parting, especially since the war was not over. Who knew when they would see one another again? Although Janez Šiško felt sorry that he wouldn't see his patient any more, he was very satisfied nonetheless that he had helped cure one of his most badly wounded patients and was returning him to his family.

At the leave-taking, Janez and Pappy exchanged addresses. In remembrance, Carl gave Janez a walking cane with the Partisan and American flags carved on it.

Peace finally arrived, and Carl Lannier joined his family in Whittier, California. But he kept his promise. It was at the end of 1945 when Janez received a letter from the United States from Pappy. In the long letter he described in detail his experiences from the time he had left the hospital until he had returned home. He had had an operation on his leg and had completely recuperated. He expressed his gratitude to all of the people who had helped him get well.

Following are excerpts from his first letter to Janez:

> I want to tell you how I returned to Italy. Also, you must tell me what happened to you after I left.
>
> It took me 14 days to arrive at the airport, and then I had to wait another 10 days for the plane. It caused me great pain to walk; although I was not strong enough, I somehow managed to overcome the strain.
>
> I was exhausted when I finally reached Captain Sayers of the British Mission. He was the one that kept sending books to me. A really fine man. He also took care of me and arranged for a Russian plane to take me to Italy.
>
> I landed in Italy on October 11. I waited there for a month before boarding a ship for America. I disembarked in the U.S.A. on November 12, and returned to my wife on December 1.
>
> I can never be grateful enough to you for saving my life. We are both very grateful to you. If you see any of my other friends, give them my regards.
>
> Just today I received a letter from Peter [the other airman who had bailed out above Bohor]. I have sent him your address and told him to write to you. He's also in the Army. When you write to me, Janez, send me the exact location where our plane had crashed, so

Photo sent to Janez Šiško of Carl Lannier and his daughter in the USA.

that I will be able to inform the parents of the boys that had been buried there. I think they will come to see the graves. If you can, mark the spot where it happened on a map. I will be very grateful to you. That will mean a lot to their relatives.

Well, Janez, I will mail this to you now and will be waiting to hear from you. Write real soon, and tell me how you are. Give my best regards to all my friends there. I sincerely hope this finds you in the very best of health and may God bless you and be with you always.

Your everlasting friend,

Pappy

PS: Do you still have your walking cane with the names on it? I have mine and will keep it forever.

Letters were exchanged from both sides of the Atlantic. Lannier also sent many supply packages that were received with appreciation, as living conditions remained difficult in post-war Europe. But Carl — "Joe" from California — stopped writing a few years later after his wife died.

After the war, Janez Šiško continued occupying himself with herbal plants and successfully helped many sick people. Without proper medical equipment and support and in unbearable and unbelievable conditions, he had saved many a life. He died in Ljubljana; I met him only a month prior to his death. Even during our last meeting he talked about his American friend and patient, Carl "Pappy" Lannier. He never gave up hope of meeting him somewhere again.

Šiško's daughter Tanja and his grandson Tomaž still carefully keep all of his correspondence with Carl Lannier as well as all his treasured objects from those unforgettable times. All of the family, especially his 18-year-old grandson, heard the stories so often that they felt as if they had experienced it all themselves. The past also became a part of them.

During an interview for a Slovene weekly newspaper in 1973, Janez Šiško was asked how he, although badly wounded himself, was able to treat 14 wounded Partisans.

Hearing the word "penicillin," he smiled.

> Why, we didn't even have chamomile. The only medicine we had was brandy, and we were very glad to have washed and reboiled bandages. I don't know how on earth the wounds could heal. I can only tell you, in those times we knew of only one treatment for pain — patience. It was unbearable, but our people endured. It was amazing how, having been wounded and ill ourselves, we could have treated other patients. But we made it because we had to and willed it.
>
>   . . . The enemy was quite close to us, but the hospital was well hidden. We were not properly armed — all we had were two Colts and a rifle. We never did find out how the Germans located it. Rumor has it that a stranger betrayed us. Fortunately, the place had been vacated when it was attacked by 200 German troops.

Šiško indicated that the hospital had been rebuilt after the war:

> From a wild deep gorge there is an extremely narrow path amongst the hazel trees winding up an exceptionally steep slope at the end of which is the rebuilt Partisan hospital. Neither God nor man would have found it if one did not know where to search. . . .
>
>   Half of it is deep underground. It was rebuilt according to a plan designed by the surviving Partisans who were reborn there. It contains a bedroom, a kitchen, a dining room, and the hospital.

The interviewer then asked if the hospital — a living monument to their heroic men — was visited frequently. Šiško replied, "Yes, and it is worth seeing."

On March 8, 1979, Janez Šiško cordially invited Carl Lannier to his country as the U.S. World War II veterans who parachuted into Yugoslavia were preparing a group visit sometime in 1979 or 1980. Šiško stressed that conditions had changed a lot in his country. Travel by foot was unnecessary, nor would they need to sleep in the dark forests. He also stressed that there was enough food, clothing, technical services, and the like so that Lannier need not bring anything except himself, and they would certainly enjoy being together again.

It was August 13, 1979, when Carl Lannier replied in his last letter that health reasons prevented him from accepting the invitation. He already had had four operations on his throat and was preparing for another one soon. They never met again.

Maloney's original crew. Front row (l. to r.): Second Lieutenant William Birchfield (navigator), Second Lieutenant Ed Brady (pilot), Second Lieutenant Clark Fetterman (bombardier), Second Lieutenant Fred Streicher (copilot). Back row: Staff Sergeant William Kollar (gunner), Technical Sergeant Clarence Jensen (engineer), Staff Sergeant Joe Maloney (tail gunner), Staff Sergeant Waldo Akers (nose gunner), Technical Sergeant John Reilly (radioman), Staff Sergeant Arthur Fleming (ball gunner).

Chapter 5

The Third Strike

by Joseph Maloney

On Sunday, April 2, 1944, two days before my 21st birthday, our crew was called for a mission to Steyr, Austria. It had been scheduled and canceled the prior two Sundays. John Reilly, our radioman, and I had previously agreed that we would play sick to avoid the same mission on the third try, so we decided not to go to the briefing, hoping that the mission would be scrubbed. But we also realized that we could not skip the mission if there was one. Without knowing for sure where or if we were going, we kept busy loading a new gadget called "windows" or "chaff" — long metal strips — which were used to "goof up" the German radar.

We were about one hour into the flight before Reilly and I realized that we were going to Steyr. We were flying the number 6 position — left wing in the second *V* formation. When the airplane in front of us returned to our air base as a result of some malfunction, we moved up into the number 3 position — left wing in the first *V* element. This should have been a safer position, since most of the enemy's fighter planes attacked from the rear.

Prior to the flight, our original pilot, Ed Brady, had been shot down with another crew. Fred Streicher was made first pilot, and George Morrel was assigned as copilot. For some reason, the nose gunner, Akers, was not with us, and Ed O'Conner came as his replacement. On board the lead plane in our six-ship box formation was a war correspondent by the name of Newbold Noyes, Jr., from the *Sunday Star* in Washington, D.C. He wrote the story of our mission, and it was printed one week later in the April 9, 1944, edition.[2]

As we drew closer to the target — Steyr — we could see the smoke coming from the ball-bearing factory. The smoke was a result of fires from the previous waves of airplanes that had dropped their bomb loads. The flak was also heavy. Our P-47 Thunderbolt and P-38 Lightning escort fighters were engaged with German fighters elsewhere, so this left us alone over the target.

While flying straight and level on our bomb run, a Junker 88 German fighter/bomber came in low toward us at the ten o'clock position and fired a rocket, which disabled three of our four engines. We fell out of formation and trailed a stream of gasoline vapor two feet in diameter from the right fuel tank. Consequently, we could not fire through it as a tracer bullet might blow us up. I watched the Ju88 dive and then come back up to finish us off. He came in at six o'clock high and dropped down as our radioman started to fire at him from the top turret position. I kept my tail turret guns down. He apparently thought that I had been hit, because I didn't start to shoot at him until he was approximately 600 yards distant. My bullets shot his left wing off, and both men in that craft bailed out before the plane went down. I had shot down the same plane that caused us to drop out of formation!

We limped off by ourselves, out of formation, for about 45 minutes. The book on the B-24 states that it cannot fly on one engine, but somehow we did. We had always talked about going to Switzerland, but we were losing altitude too fast to fly over the Alps, so we took a route due south, hoping to reach the Adriatic Sea before bailing out. Thinking back, this could have been bad for me, as I don't swim.

But Fred Streicher, our pilot, told us to prepare to bail out then. A U.S. aircraft ahead of us was in the same general shape as we were and had 40 to 50 German fighters around it. They allowed the crew to bail out; then they shot the plane down. They then turned their attention to us. They also gave us time to bail out by flying a circle around our plane. I had previously told Fred that if we had to jump, I'd first clear the back and then inform him so he could avoid piloting the aircraft any longer than necessary. Therefore, when Fred gave the command to bail out, I cleared the other three crew members from the back and called "All clear!" over the interphone.

In crawling from the front of the plane to the bomb bay, Clark Fetterman's chute was opened accidentally and came out in his arms. Since he was afraid to jump, our radio operator pushed him out. The chute opened and worked well.

I was afraid to jump but had no choice. This was the first jump for all of us — we had no previous practice — and the first jump had to be correct. After my chute opened with a jerk, I thought my groin was in my mouth. The descent was very quiet but scary as the German planes kept circling with the pilots waving to us. I was always afraid that one might turn and shoot us while we were suspended in the air or, worse yet, that they would come in close and their prop-wash could spill our chute. If this happened we would have a free-fall to our death.

When I was close to the ground I saw that I was coming down on a farmhouse, so I slipped my chute to avoid it. Somehow I missed and hit the earth so hard that my head went to the ground and scraped my forehead. A woman came out with a pitchfork. This made her boss since I had nothing — we never carried a gun since the six bullets it held would only get us into more trouble. I could see that she was more interested in the parachute material than in me, so when she picked it up I ran for the nearby woods. On the way I met a boy who could see that I was an American, and he offered me a flask of wine, which I finished. (We later learned that our plane had crashed in the courtyard of Tolst Vrh, near Sentjernej. The crew landed near the villages of Gabrje, Stopiče, Dolze, and Vel Cerovec.)

As I neared the woods, two men emerged with machine guns. They tried to tell me that Tito was a friend. We had never been briefed on Tito, so their gestures didn't mean anything. One man walked in front of me and the other behind me, so I had to go with them. They had our crew reunited after three days, and an English-speaking Partisan explained everything to us. He stated that the Partisan movement, under the leadership of Marshal Tito, was on the side of the Allied forces and against the Germans. They would attempt to return us to our own forces and safety. Prior to being shot down, we had never been briefed on Tito or the Partisans. This was a big mistake by the U.S. Air Forces.

When we bailed out, the only clothes that we wore were the heated flying suits, which were like heavy pajamas with electric wire woven into the cloth. The flight boots were similar. The suits were bright blue and would stand out; the boots were not for walking. The Partisans took the clothing off of their backs and shoes from their feet so that we could travel. This was a real sacrifice on their part, because the only food and clothing that they had was obtained by raiding the Germans. Without saying a word, they shared everything with us.

The Partisans moved us from village to village, walking single file in groups of five or six, with a small distance between groups. I am told that the reason for this was to avoid all of us being attacked at the same time.

As we traveled we kept adding additional evadees until we numbered 81. It was the largest single group that they had ever moved. One of the newcomers was a Frenchman who had been taken prisoner when the French Navy capitulated. He joined our group after escaping from a camp. It was strange that no one else of the other 80 persons spoke a word of French. We were concerned that he might be a plant, so we always stood guard over him. He turned out to be all right.

Our group included three Englishmen who were taken prisoner in North Africa and moved to a camp in Germany. They had also escaped and joined us in hoping for freedom. Two of our group came from India, and they gave us problems. Their religion did not allow them to eat many things that the rest of us ate. I recall that we were in trouble when they stole some chickens to eat but would not admit to it. We also had a Russian man and woman accompany us for a short time — perhaps five days; they came from out of nowhere and left the same way. We suspected they were spies and called them "Search" and "Record." We were not happy to have them with us and were glad when they left.

Every day was dangerous and risky, but on April 19 it got worse. On that morning we were coming into a village after walking all night. Word came that we were going to have eggs and pancakes for breakfast for the first time since being shot down. We entered the village from one direction, and a German patrol came in from another. This very quickly changed our lives. They soon had small planes flying over us while firing machine guns and throwing hand grenades.

After a period of time we made it into the woods and walked around the village. We regrouped and started down a long, straight road when a Ju88 suddenly appeared above us. As we all dove for the sides of the road, I found myself next to the radio operator. We held hands and said good-bye to each other, ending, "I'll see you in the next place." We were scared that we were all going to be strafed and killed. But the German pilot must not have seen us, as he flew directly over us and kept going.

We started walking again and came to a river that was being patrolled by a small plane. The Partisans hid us in a farmhouse, and they timed the plane as it went up and down the river. They took all 81 of us across the river in a rowboat — three at a time — and hid us in the woods on the opposite side, then returned the boat to its original position so that everything appeared to be the same each time the small plane went over. Later that same afternoon we were moved in trucks to another village where we rested.

At dusk we climbed over a nearby mountain and down into a valley on the other side where we were to cross a German railway. As we came close to the tracks, we could see that the Germans were patrolling the area with small hand-cars and shooting up flares that descended on parachutes to light the area. It was as bright as our noonday sun. After a waiting period, it was evident that we could not make the crossing, so we retraced our trip back over the mountain to the village of Podgrad.

The village was located at the closed end of a long, horseshoe-shaped valley. At daylight, April 20, we entered a house and noticed a woman cooking a potato and warming a cup of milk over a fire in the middle of the floor. The house had no stove or chimney. The fire was burning on the dirt floor, and the smoke escaped through a hole in the roof. Before the food was ready, I heard machine guns firing and bullets hitting the buildings. The gunfire came from German troops and the *Bela Garda,* or "White Guards," Yugoslav natives allied with the Germans. We all ran from the houses across the closed end of the valley, hoping to get into the woods. As we started up the mountain, we found it ringed with Germans and White Guards, so we could run the length of the valley only. All this time, we were out in the open with no place to hide.

While we were running, my pilot, Fred Streicher, was hit in the right calf and fell back into a ditch a few feet from me with the upper part of his body in a gully and his leg up high. From later accounts supplied by his wife, Eileen, an English soldier — believed to be Hillary King — was the first to arrive and applied a makeshift tourniquet to stop or slow the bleeding somewhat; he then continued on his way. Copilot George Morrel stopped to help, but Fred told him to leave. George started to run but had gone only a few feet when a bullet hit him in the back and killed him instantly. The Germans came along, and one of them beat Fred with his gun butt. Fred passed out very quickly, and when he came to, another soldier was methodically going through his pockets. The soldier took Fred's wallet and watch, then removed George's shirt and put it on Fred. It is assumed that George is buried near this village. Fred was taken prisoner and put in the back of a covered wagon. (Reportedly, the Germans did not take POWs as a normal practice during this period of the war.) As he was hauled away, he could hear gunshots and see smoke coming from the village. (About a day or so after the remainder of our group of 81 returned to Italy on May 2, I was told that the Germans paratroopers landed in the last village of our stay and killed every person in the town for helping us. To date I have not been able to verify this.)

Fred was repeatedly questioned by the Germans, "Streicher, Streicher, how can you bomb your own people?" Fred would reply that he was an American officer following orders. Two or three days later, they arrived at a German field hospital — a barn. A German doctor examined him and told him that gangrene had set in and his leg would have to come off. When Fred questioned the decision, the medic assured him that he was first a doctor, then a German. They had almost nothing in the way of medicine. They removed his leg without anesthesia or antibiotics. At that time Fred was in so much pain that he immediately passed out.

Fred was later moved to different POW camps — some good, some bad. While in one of these camps, they had to re-amputate his leg because it became infected again. His leg was removed above the knee. (After the war he was fitted with an artificial leg and learned to fly airplanes and water ski!)

During the action when Fred was hit, the Frenchman who had joined our original group grabbed a pair of horses hooked to a wagon and drove it like a Roman chariot as he went by me. After traveling only a few more yards, he hit a bump and was thrown off. Almost immediately, a mortar shell landed between the horses and blew them and the wagon apart. When he fell off, it saved his life.

Maloney with Mrs. Ana Brodarec, who was in the resistance movement in Yugoslavia and who helped Maloney research the events of 1944.

For the remainder of that day and into the night, those of us remaining ran or walked to put some distance between us and the Germans. First we had to run the length of the valley — perhaps two or three miles long — and then into the woods for protection. We were constantly on the move. It is not easy to move such a large group of persons, but the brave Partisans did just that without any question for their own safety.

One day the Partisans caught a White Guard who was going to turn us in. They walked him beside us, beating him with a gun butt. They wanted us to do it as well, but we could not. Later that same evening, when we were about to cross a railway, they decided to kill him. A gunshot would have been too noisy, so they cut his throat just as I was going by — perhaps 10 to 15 feet away. I will always remember that sound.

One day blended into another while we were there, and I did not know the dates until later. At the time, the most important thing was to leave safely. We later walked to Podgrad, the place where we had been attacked earlier. From there we traveled for about a week to the grass field used by the Partisans as an airport near the town of Metlika, located between the villages of Otok and Podzemelj. An English outpost was located at the site with a radio to contact Bari, Italy, the 98th Bomb Group headquarters. A short time after the contact was made, they sent aircraft to evacuate us. One day while waiting for the arrival of the Allied planes, we were bombed by German aircraft.

Only one C-47 was able to land due to the fog. (The Army Air Forces could not land planes to evacuate the remainder until a week later, after the fog lifted.) In a way, I was lucky — my feet were infected, and since the Partisans were afraid of gangrene, I was scheduled to leave on the first plane out. I was taken by horse and wagon to the aircraft on April 29 for the trip to the Army hospital in Bari, where my feet received the proper medical treatment. Due to malnourishment, I was awakened every two hours and fed small amounts of food. After debriefing, I was released from the hospital and given travel orders to return to the U.S. using any method of transportation available. Traveling was difficult since the timing coincided with the invasion of France. Everything was in an uproar.

From Bari I returned to my base in Leece, Italy, where I learned that I was the first person in our group to have been shot down and returned.

During the period that we spent behind enemy lines, I don't remember that we ever removed our clothes or shoes; we lived and slept in them. We could wash only in streams and could never brush our teeth. In one village, a man offered to shave all of us. Everyone was afraid to be first, but he was okay.

I do not consider myself to be superstitious, but we were shot down on the third attempt to bomb the same target and were also scheduled on a Sunday every time; was there a warning similar to the baseball expression "three times out"? Also, when we walked at night, there was not much to do but watch the sky. It seems that every time we saw a falling or shooting star we made the trip safely, but on a dark, cloudy night we would run into trouble. I still watch for falling stars.

Chapter 6

An Airman's Diary of His Rescue

On May 9, 1944, a squadron of Flying Fortresses from the 463rd Bomb Group stationed in Foggia, Italy, prepared for a bombing mission to the aircraft factories and ball-bearing manufacturing plants in Wiener Neuestadt, Austria. The mission was scrapped until the next day due to unfavorable weather conditions. As the Americans prepared once again on the following day, May 10, the enemy had plenty of time to plan for countermeasures after their spy's message was relayed to them. While the Americans were over the target zones, they were attacked by a large force of German fighter aircraft that succeeded in destroying quite a number of the Allied planes.

A crew member in one of the planes shot down on that day was Second Lieutenant Loryn E. McQuerter. It was his twenty-fifth sortie against the enemy. His plane had been attacked by four German fighters and riddled with bullets. Three of the ten crew members were killed by flak, and four of the remaining seven who bailed out were never accounted for. Loryn was one of the three survivors who parachuted to safety, near Pohorje.

Loryn landed in a meadow between two wooded hills at 11:30 a.m. After he hurriedly removed the chute he heard far-off voices and crept into some nearby dense shrubbery. Soon afterward, some German troops and collaborating civilians approached his hiding place. They picked up his chute but only searched about half of the surrounding area. Luckily, Loryn was well camouflaged, and they did not find him. However, after they left, he did not dare leave his hiding place, and he slept there overnight.

As dawn approached, he heard bells ringing and discovered it was caused by the cows which were grazing peacefully quite close to him. Scrutinizing the scenery much closer, he saw a woman 60 to 70 years of age working in the field. Although she noticed him immediately, he had the impression that he was not welcome. He stepped toward the cows gingerly as he had injured his knee while landing. There behind the cows he saw a 10- or 12-year-old boy with his finger to his lips signaling that McQuerter should be quiet and remain where he was. Shortly thereafter the boy motioned for Loryn to follow him to the house. En route Loryn learned that he was not in Austria but in Yugoslavia. Leading him through the back door, he was greeted heartily by an elderly man of about 80 who welcomed him and offered him some brandy and food. They did not talk much as Loryn knew only English.

After staying overnight, one of the local inhabitants guided him toward an adjacent wooded area. As they approached, the guide stopped and clapped his hands, a signal for a woman dressed in black who emerged from the woods and motioned for Loryn to follow her. She walked very fast, and Loryn had difficulty in keeping up with her due to his injured leg.

They walked for a long time before the woman stopped and clapped her hands three times. Three men appeared. They had no uniforms or even Partisan caps. They continued their hike until they arrived at another house. After a short wait, a woman with a basket of food appeared.

Everything was conducted in silence and with an air of mystery. While nobody attempted to converse with Loryn, they were very attentive and treated him kindly. The following day he felt relieved when he met some Partisans who were armed and in uniform. He felt even better when one of them, Ciril Dolenc (Partisan name: "Ciko"), an officer from the 4th Operative Zone, spoke good English. They became friendly at once, and Loryn's hopes increased for a happy ending to his odyssey. Ciko assumed personal responsibility for the American, bringing him safely through some dangerous territory, including crossing the Sava River, before reaching the vicinity of a liberated zone.

It was an emotional parting for both of them. Loryn exchanged his Colt automatic for Ciko's Partisan pistol. Ciko also gave Loryn a photo of himself together with a Partisan pass issued to the American airman by the 4th Operative Zone. While treasuring the artifacts for over 30 years after the war, Loryn often wondered how to thank the good people who had helped him, especially Ciko.

Some years later when he visited Europe, Loryn decided to visit the area where he had been rescued. As he crossed the Austrian border to enter Yugoslavia near Dravograd, he presented his old Partisan pass along with his passport to the customs officer and the military officer on duty. By coincidence, the head of the border crossing was Aleksander Borštnar, the brother of Jože Borštnar who had signed the 1944 Partisan pass. It caused an immediate party atmosphere. The border authorities hospitably invited Loryn's entire

Ciril Dolenc, "Ciko," the Partisan officer who took care of Loryn McQuerter.

family to a small reception. In addition, Loryn discovered that the back side of Ciko's photograph included his home address in Ljubljana. Loryn had thought that the writing was simply a statement of their friendship. After his initial surprise, he lost no time driving directly to Ljubljana, the capital of Slovenia, where he arrived late at night. He registered at the Hotel Slon, eagerly awaiting the next day.

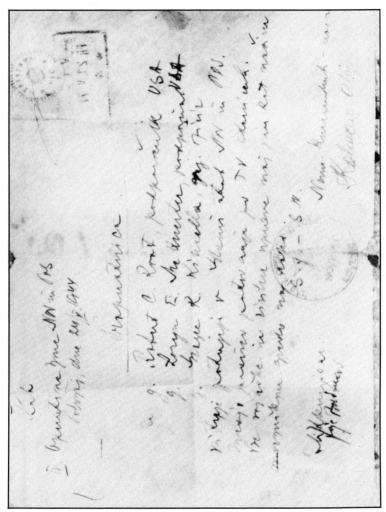

The Partisan pass, issued in 1944, created a pleasant surprise when presented 35 years later at the Yugoslavian border.

Loryn McQuerter (at left) with his wife, daughter, son-in-law, and a friend from Lju-bljana.

Loryn and his family set out early the next morning. They first stopped at an inn, Pri Jerneju (At Jerry's), where they showed Ciko's photo to the people there. While the innkeeper did not know the individual, a casual bystander recognized the Partisan at once. Unfortunately, she had to inform them that Ciko had been killed in the last month of the war. The news staggered Loryn, who was unprepared to accept the fact that his good friend was dead. The main reason that he and his family had traveled specifically to Ljubljana was their strong desire to personally thank Ciko for his unselfish support during those difficult times during the war.

However, they learned of Ciko's sister who lived nearby, resulting in a touching meeting. They were joined by Ciko's pre-war friend and military comrade Vitomil Zupan, who spoke sufficient English so that they talked late into the night. The following day they went sightseeing in Ljubljana and then drove to Cirmen's in Medno, 10 to 15 kilometers northwest of Ljubljana, where another surprise awaited them.

I learned from fellow journalists that Loryn, the rescued airman, was in Medno, and thus I brought my archives of Partisan photographs, including some Allied photos as well. I also brought some papers and the Research Institute Ljubljana's list, "Allied Airmen and Prisoners of War Rescued by the Slovene Partisans," which documented Loryn's name and other data under #75.

Before parting, I asked Loryn what his most vivid memories were of those hard times. He did not answer at once. There was a long silence while he was deep in thought, then he started to answer slowly:

> I was parachuting into an unknown area that I anticipated would be hostile. I expected to be apprehended by the enemy and I knew I would be in danger. The place where I landed was beautiful, like Eden itself, but I couldn't spend time enjoying the scenery or congratulating myself on my safe landing and not being shot. I was quite prepared to take the necessary precautions to avoid being surprised. It soon paid off when I heard voices in an unfamiliar language.

Loryn's wife, Abie, followed her husband's comments: "I had no knowledge of what my husband went through. Two days after he bailed out I gave birth to our son Kent. I am most happy and grateful to all who helped him."

Their daughter, an assistant professor at a California university, added, "I could never have imagined that my father had lived here among so many warm-hearted people during the war."

Before concluding his visit, Loryn was interested in learning the identity and whereabouts of the young boy who had been the first one to lead him to safety. Thanks to him, Loryn's story had a happy ending. He wanted to shake the hand of the lad, who by now would be about 45 years old, and express his most deep-felt gratitude. He offered to return to Europe at another time just to meet the boy, but unfortunately, in spite of appeals in various newspapers, his identity was never revealed.

The American Airman's Diary

During Loryn McQuerter's stay with the Partisans, he had written in a diary, which he brought with him during his 1979 visit. It contained many initials instead of names to protect various individuals in the event that he was captured, wounded, or killed (for example, *P* for Partisans, *G* for Germans, etc.). While some of the descriptions and names of town and villages are not technically correct, I made very few corrections in order to preserve the document's authenticity. Corrections are noted within brackets.

* * * * *

May 10, 1944, Wednesday — Bailed out at 4,000 feet at 1200 to the north of Marboua Yugo [Maribor]. Jumped down on a small field at the foot of a hill. Folded the chute and ran to the forest. Hid boots, a chute and my Mae West life preserver under a tree stump and found a near-by hiding place for myself.

Most of the morning stayed there and would have stayed longer if not for rain. Somewhere nearby I heard some talking. Later learned that the Germans had found my chute and other hidden things. At about 1700 I caught sight of a woman in the field and tried to approach her. She could not help me anyway except to motion me to a nearby house. Saw cows and a boy herder in the field. That boy took me to the house, gave me some wine, an omelette and a comfortable bed where I slept overnight. Have a pain in my knee; I hurt it during the jump.

May 11, Thursday — Hid in the forest for some time; an elderly man came to see me from time to time. He understood my wish. An hour later he took me to a woman and left me. The woman rushed through the woods; it was hardly possible to follow her, especially up the hill. She hid me. A little later two Partisans came and took me to a place where there were some more Partisans. Mac and Root were there too [Robert C. Root and George R. Kinsel, two of his crew members who were also rescued]. Stayed in the forest for the whole afternoon.

May 12, Friday — Stayed in the forest most of the night and then went to the barn to sleep on hay. Later we were given goulash to eat. Stayed in the forest all day, but had blankets. Women brought us food and we were given tobacco. About dusk we started walking. Sure a rough trip. Thought I could never make it. About dark we met a P[artisan] brigade and they gave Mac a horse. Mac's leg was injured. We traveled on for a while and came to a house where we stopped and ate and were given beds of straw on the floor. Could hear shots down the mountain from here.

May 13, Saturday — Started out about daybreak and walked to where part of a brigade was housed. Had some coffee and rested awhile, then continued on our way with the P[artisans]. In the afternoon we reached the brigade headquarters. Stayed there all day.

May 14, Sunday — Slept on the floor — could hardly eat the food. Began our journey about 1700. Walked to the first R.R. and road. Were in a house eating and had an alert and had to run in the forest and hide. After dark we slipped through the G[erman] patrols and on into the darkness and the mountains. Walked to about 0200 when we reached a P[artisan] station. Slept in the barn on the hay.

May 15, Monday — Had two alerts this day. Had to run out of the house and up the mountain and hide. The second time more shots were fired. One bullet went through the house [window] we learned later. Didn't go back to the house the second time but continued on our way for awhile. Walked until after dark and stopped at a house where there were two women. We were starving by now. Had their coffee for breakfast and a little food at noon.

May 16, Tuesday — Slept on a bench in the old house. Had hot milk and bread for supper and breakfast. Very hungry. Very cold. Started out that morning and stopped at another dirty house. More P[artisans] came and went for food. Had meat cooking when we had an alert and went to the forest. We were surrounded by G[ermans]. Couldn't get out that night. Tried to and three shots were fired at us. Lay in the forest all night in the rain. Shots were fired around us all night.

May 17, Wednesday — Moved to another place in the forest and hid all day. About dusk we slipped out. Stopped at a house and had a little coffee and bread. Climbed the mountain and stopped at a house. Had bread and wine. Could hear shots on down the mountain.

May 18, Thursday — Just lay down on the floor of the house for some much needed rest when we had an alert. Ran out in a heavy rain and finally in the barn. Stayed until about 0300 and started out. Walked to about noon to a house. Had some food that we could hardly eat. House was worse than a barn.

May 19, Friday — Stayed there until about 0300 and started out. Chica [a guide] came to help us. Tried to cross a road but couldn't. Had some food in the woods where we stayed until dusk, then headed back to the station that we had left Monday. Got there that night and had some tea.

May 20, Saturday — Still at station going nuts. Food terrible and poor sleeping on a bench. Waiting for the blockade to move so that we can get through.

May 21, Sunday — Still at same place. Had a big bowl of beans and got

A typical crossing — the Kolpa River in the vicinity of a Partisan airfield.

sick. Very tired of place and no tobacco. The family got dressed and went to church. Dress sure plain. Had some eggs today cooked in so much grease could hardly eat them. (Cree became ill.)

May 22, Monday — Day as usual but started out six in the evening hearing the road was clear.

May 23, Tuesday — We walked like mad last night all night, stopping once in awhile for little food along the way. Somewhere the G[ermans] had been with blockades. Stopped at 0600 and slept in a bed — for the first time — till 1200. Had some good food and were on our way.

May 24, Wednesday — At 2400 last night we stopped at a nice house after crossing the [Sava] river. Very nice people — two girls and a mother got up. Had cigarettes, wine, brandy, and some sweet bread and coffee. Very good. Had good bed.

May 25, Thursday — Good night's rest last night and good food. Started out for [Zone] station about 1200 and got there about 1800. Saw English major. He knew nothing about us getting out.

May 26, Friday — Stayed at station and had good bed last night and good food, meat. Chica left us here. Started with new guide about 1500 and walked to 2200. Stopped on way for food. Got some brown bread and clabbered milk and some coffee.

May 27, Saturday — Started out about 0700 after spending a cold night on the bench. Had some eggs for breakfast, but so much grease on them we could hardly eat them. Walked until about 1000 and hid in the woods with one [Iti] and two injured men until about 1700. Walked until 2400 and had some coffee and bread. Slept until 0300 on bench.

May 28, Sunday — Started out at 0300. Stopped at a house full of children. Had coffee and brown mush and slept on bench till 1200 and started out again. Went to station and rested on grass. Ate at 1400 and rested till 1730 and started out. Crossed the [Sava] river in a boat after waiting awhile in the brush. The boat tipped over on one fellow and he got all wet. Also crossed R.R. and road. Trains went by while we were in the brush. Had to wade part of the river. There were about 30 in our outfit — one girl — all with big packs. At first I could hardly climb the mountains and keep going, but getting in pretty good shape now. Have lost about 3" in waist and most of my bottom. I thought I was pretty strong so offered to carry the girl's pack. It surely weighed 50 pounds. I made it until about 2400 and had to give it back. I didn't know we were going to walk all night. I carried the pack too long. I almost didn't make it. We stopped one place and got some raw fat bacon and brown bread. I couldn't eat mine. About dawn we came through the barb wire — the front line. We walked on until 0700. I was dead tired but in liberated territory.

This morning at 0700 we arrived back in civilization after walking all night. Sure was tired and sleepy. We came down from the mountains into this valley and village of S[emič]. The church bells and chimes were sounding and people in their Sunday best were walking to church. There were two or three large churches here. We stopped at the edge of the village and had some brandy and tea. The houses are much nicer here. More like the U.S. We then went to P[artisan] headquarters and after waiting awhile, went upstairs where an officer and family lived and had fried eggs, rolls, and tea. I can't describe how good they were. After awhile they brought a fellow that spoke English — had been in the U.S. two years. Then a hack was brought for us to ride in! We were taken on down the road to a house and sort of a hotel, where we were to stay and rest. Nice house and hotel — separate building. The man is a big fat jolly good fellow. What a day we've had! Had fried eggs again and then to bed. Nice bed with clean sheets and everything. I have a private room. Got us to eat a wonderful dinner at 1800 — fried potatoes, pork chops, wine, salad, cinnamon loaf, and coffee, and then turnovers for dessert. What a feast! After eating we started for a little barber shop and were invited by two women in their backyard to have wine and cinnamon loaf. They were very nice. These people are the best I've ever met. Finally we got to the barber shop and beauty shop — run by two women. I got my second shave since May 10, haircut and shampoo — all for 20 lire [100 lire = $1]. It was all grand. This morning we got 100 Yugoslavian cigarettes — [$2.50]. That was grand too. This afternoon

Transporting wounded airmen and Partisans.

we were surprised by three American soldiers — major, lieutenant, and sergeant — and three English. They were going north. Tough. They gave us a carton of cigarettes and some more supplies — one toothbrush that we'll all use. This has been a wonderful day. Must get in this fine bed and will start writing of the trip later. It's sure nice and quiet here — no noise. A beautiful night. I'm thankful to be alive. Would give anything in the world if Abie could be here.

May 29, Monday — Had a good night's sleep — in a good bed. Got up about 0730 for breakfast. Was looking around the bombed R.R. tracks when U.S. bombers began coming over 0800-1000. The people all got out in the road and one lady just jumped up and down with joy. I talked the best I could with her and her husband and another well-dressed man, and they invited me in the house for wine and food. Stayed most of the morning with them. Dinner was almost ready when we had an alert and had to leave quickly. There was a hack for us and we went outside the village to another house, where we waited and had more eggs and wine. Later we started south in the cart. Stopped in another village for wine in sort of a saloon-town pub. On our way again, we had to walk around some places where the road had been blocked. Finally got to the zone headquarters where we had supper. Not bad, and stayed for the night in a school house on straw.

May 30, Tuesday — A cart came for us about 0900 and we began our journey south. The cart turned over twice, but no injuries. We traveled over some very rough road — the roughest ride I've ever taken — until noon. (Saw our bombers go over again — 0800-1000.) Stopped for food at noon. One big bowl of potatoes, beans and meat — not bad. But I had such a jolting in the hot sun I couldn't eat much. Traded carts two or three times and finally got two horses and springs on cart — much better. We reach [Semič] about 0600. I had a terrific headache. Here there is another U.S. boy. Has been here a long time. Had his arm shot off, but seems to be doing okay. Nice boy. Sergeant on a B-17.

May 31, Wednesday — Ill and vomited last night before supper and couldn't eat much — too greasy. Corn mush and gravy broth. Had a pretty good bed — covered straw on the floor, with a blanket. The food is terrible here. This morning went up to the village pub and had some good wine. Beans and potatoes cooked together for dinner. This afternoon a British captain and American captain came and gave us some cigarettes, soap, socks, and underwear. They say we'll be here for several days. The captain is supposed to help us but he waited plenty too long to come. He's a lot of wind. The English captain was a nice fellow. Thank goodness, I do have a little reading here that [Leo] has. The food is terrible here. Went with [Leo] for a walk and stopped at the pub and wine. To bed early.

June 1, Thursday — A red letter day — had a wonderful bath and clean woolens. [English] went after more wine. Helped Leo take a bath. P[artisans] came with supplies. Read. Food awful. Weather very nice here. Sure like to leave.

June 2, Friday — A runner came and said we were leaving today. English captain came about noon with more supplies. Had a very good dinner. Walked until about 1800. Stopped on the road for wine. Had meat and potatoes at [Metlika]. Got a room where the man can speak English. Had been to America. Had wine and good ham with him.

June 3, Saturday — Had a very good room and bed. Raining this morning. Rained until about noon. Stayed all day in [Metlika]. Had quite a visit with Joe. Speaks good English. Whiskey before breakfast. He asked me for breakfast and dinner — good food. He gave me a picture of their church. Got a shave today. Slept a lot. No more rain. Will probably move on tomorrow. Good bed here where both [Itis] and [Jerries] have slept.

June 4, Sunday — Had a good night's sleep. The lady here is very nice and a good cook. Churned butter just for me. Ate bread, butter, and wine last night till 2300. Walked about six hours today. Stopped and had a mixture of beans and few potatoes. In [Croatia] now — will stay here for tonight. Have a new guide. These are the poorest people we've seen. Didn't have supper until 2200. Corn bread with grease over it. Terrible food.

June 5, Monday — Slept on some musty hay on floor of dirty house. The people are awful dirty here in C[roatia]. Didn't sleep very well. Got up at 0700. At 0900 had corn bread and some greasy water and started out. Walked till 1500 and stopped and asked for food. People brought out wine (good) and corn bread and milk. The bread was terrible. Sat there and ate milk and bread in the road by the barn and cow manure. All out of one pan, as usual. The people all gathered to watch us — as usual. Walked until 1700 — very hot here. Stopped in a village, but had to run up a hill. There was a skirmish between the C[roatian] Guards and the P[artisans]. At 2100 we started — [50] strong. Very pretty moon-lit night. Crossed the main highway and R.R. into [Zagreb]. Walked in valley after 2200 — big valley. Hungry. Walked all night.

June 6, Tuesday — The hardest trip we've had. Stopped to rest and ate some rations (corn beef) the English captain gave us. At 0900 this morning stopped and slept along the road. Lady gave us some milk and corn bread — terrible. Moved in the woods at 1300 and stayed until 1500. A little food there — and moved on. Terrible day. We're at some old house now. Probably for the night. Very poor country. Later: Went to another house and lady had eggs for us. Not very good. They ruin everything here. Assigned to the barn for the night.

June 7, Wednesday — Had a cold night in the barn. No cover. Also, fleas terrible. Had breakfast at the same lady's house — bread, milk and some meat cracklings. I ate no meat. We were very anxious to leave today, but the darn Iti

B-24 over Partisan territory.

said he wasn't able, so we spent a miserable day in the barn. The old lady tries to please us at meals though, but they just don't have anything. Would give anything to get going. This is the poorest [escort] we've had.

June 8, Thursday — Rained about all night last night. Had potatoes and onions for supper last night. Another cold, fleay night in the barn. Walked till three — off and on. (Rested too much.) Stopped at a place to eat. Terrible place — potatoes and eggs — we collected the eggs. Food not too bad but the poorest country yet. Some of the houses little squares — mud, with hay and corn on top. Everybody barefooted. Poorest people I've ever seen. In the so-called village now. Every building but one destroyed. Waiting to see what they're going to do with us. Possible that we leave tonight, but know we couldn't. Would give anything to leave. Supposed to be a village near here where we can leave from. (In Italy — delayed.) The old man here speaks some English. Took us in and asked us what we wanted. He had only milk and no one could drink any — the place was so dirty and had such an odor. We told him to get us the guide — we wanted to leave. He did — walked about an hour real fast and came to a house where there were some 25 American fliers and two [New Zealand] and 2 Australian and 3 diplomats — Hungary, etc. Sure enough there was supposed to be a plane in about 2400. Some dropped supplies and one landed. There was just a field there and no one had landed before. Had been landing about 4 days south. But have to move around.

Everyone had already eaten so we finished the rations we had been carrying. The whole room was covered with hay and I managed to find a small area. (More time now so more details.) About 2300 we heard planes and ran out. Everyone was crazy to leave there. Sure enough we could see them dropping supplies in the distance. The American captain that was supposed to be there with the signal lights wasn't, so we just knew that no one would land. We all ran for straw and dimly lighted a runway anyway. Sure enough there came a plane over low and came in to land. He was down immediately but overshot and ran over the hill, nearly missing a big ditch and stopped in a swamp just short of a big bank. Luck! But our hopes of leaving that night were gone.

June 9, Friday — We ran all over the hill to the C-47 and luckily found that no one was hurt and no apparent damage to the plane, but it was almost to the wing in mud and one prop had bit in [to the ground]. About 0300 I went to the house. My right knee hurt considerably. I had sprained it the day before and also had fallen that night while running to the plane. I had been on the hay scratching fleas [earlier for] a short time when [all] came. The Partisans were cutting trees to camouflage [the plane] the next day. Oh, yes, the pilot (a captain — very nice) and his crew passed out American cigarettes — very good. We were to try to get the plane out during the day. I couldn't go to sleep — the fellows on both sides of me snoring terribly and some stinker's feet against my head and the fleas. I got up and gave someone else my spot and sat up the rest of the night. Daylight soon came. After a cup of hot milk we went to the plane — a sorry position she was in but a good sight. The boys dug out around the wheel and got some boards to make a [stable base]. About 1500, 23 teams of oxen were there. The natives finally got them hooked to the plane. Quite a sight. The first lunge and push by the men moved the plane. There was hope. By 1830 after much strain and breakage by oxen, the plane was on level ground. Now for the check. The crew chiefs reported okay — 2400 was take-off. We then had a little to eat. I had a terrible headache. No one could sleep, but all gathered around the airplane and waited. There was to be another drop that night and maybe a plane would land so that everyone could be taken out. The planes came again and we lit the fires outlining a runway — a different one — but none landed. So the word was given to get in and get set. [There was] a rush — 26 was a normal load and we had 34 wanting to go. Some diplomats and the [Iti] were left. 31 loaded — in a plane that we knew was capable of it if there were no unforeseen damage and on a suitable runway. The captain could hardly refuse anyone. We were taking off downhill with flaps and brakes [set] before the take-off. The pilot said he thought he could make it. We did. You can imagine the tenseness on take-off!

June 10, Saturday — I had tried to vomit to ease my headache before leaving but nothing there. It eased somewhat on the plane. At 0300 we — a very happy, thankful group — landed at [Bari] field. At 0430 we were at the hospital. After some red tape we were assigned to a good tent and cot and blankets and P.J.'s. Breakfast in an hour, but we were served some coffee and a sandwich and a tired body dropped in bed. I knew I wouldn't get up in an hour for breakfast, but did get up at 0800 and had a good shower and lunch at 1100, with good white bread. I could have enjoyed a meal of just that. The shower was wonderful, too. We hadn't been up an hour until the Red Cross came in with a bundle — towel, hanky, soap, toothbrush, tooth powder, razor and blades, and shaving cream, three packages of cigarettes, two candy bars, 1 package gum, and perhaps something else — I can't recall at present. From now on they get my praise as ever. Twice today they brought us reading material. We were also permitted to get our P.X. rations today. Nice big hospital here at [Bari]. It hasn't been bombed. It's pretty here. Sure looks good to us. I weighed today — 148 pounds — a loss of about 22 pounds overseas, and most of it in the last 31 days. My pants just hang on me. This has been a wonderful day. Only by the grace of God could such a day be made possible. Of course, I'm expecting to get to go see my dear wife and baby. Think I haven't before mentioned that the American major in [   ] gave us [40,000] lire and the English captain [9,000] lire. For my part, I have about [$12] worth left and, of the $48 in the escape kit, I traded $30 for $45 worth of lire, and have about [$12] of it left, so I am about [$70] richer than when I started. Not bad! Have been reading today and am going to see "Private Hargrove" tonight. Will leave here tomorrow.

June 11, Sunday — Had a very good night's sleep last night. Today about 1000 went over to the Q.M. [quartermaster] and got some clothes. Had fried chicken for dinner and then was taken to headquarters for interrogation. Got nothing out of them about going home. Wanted to go to squadron tonight but no transportation. Supposed to go in the morning. Sure hope I get to go home. Heard today that Abie should get word of my safety in 36 hours. I sure hope so.

* * * * *

Loryn McQuerter did indeed make it home.

Dr. Vinko Dom-
itrovič aided seri-
ously wounded
airmen. After the
war he was one
of the consulting
surgeons during
Marshal Tito's ill-
ness.

Chapter 7

Tragedy on Velika Planina

"Allied Airmen and Prisoners of War Rescued by the Slovene Partisans" includes the names of William M. Lesser from Sacramento, California, and Charles L. Wensley from Austin, Texas. The publication reports that their B-17 Flying Fortress crashed on May 29, 1944, on the slopes of Velika Planina (5,465 feet above sea level), a mountain in the Kamniške Alps, and that the two airmen were rescued by the Partisans and escorted to the Bela Krajina area, from where they flew back to Italy on July 19, 1944.

I knew about those facts for some years as I was preparing material to use in my second book on rescued airmen. However, I did not succeed then in finding anyone who could give me more information about that particular incident.

One Sunday morning as I listened to the radio program "Do You Still Remember, Comrades?," my attention was drawn to a dialogue between the radio reporter and a Partisan physician, Vinko Domitrovič (he was one of the surgeons consulted at the time of Marshal Tito's illness). Domitrovič mentioned that he had treated an American airman during the war. The thought occurred to me that perhaps I could obtain some information about the events that happened 42 years previous. Domitrovič was now retired and lived at the foothill of Smarna Gora, a mountain near Ljubljana. Since I used to climb there almost every day, it was not difficult for me to arrange a visit and continue the discussion on this subject. He related the following.

* * * * *

During that period I was an assistant medical orderly with the Slandrova Brigade. During the middle of the night, someone from a nearby post and unknown to me demanded immediate medical help — a doctor. I was summoned by the staff and, without any further explanation or information, ordered to accompany the stranger immediately. Taking only the fundamental medical equipment, the courier and I departed that night and proceeded to our "unknown" destination. We walked all night, passing Kamniška Bistrica and heading for Jezersko. We finally stopped at a tent under some tall fir trees. Local Partisans and couriers were inside together with three American airmen who had just parachuted from their airplane before it crashed. One, called "Captain" by the other two, was the most seriously injured. I diagnosed spinal fracture with two broken shinbones; he remained conscious. The second flier appeared to be satisfactory except that he was so exhausted he couldn't stand. The third one was more or less well. One of the Partisans called "Chicago" had lived in America for a while and acted as our interpreter. I immediately administered first aid until the arrival shortly thereafter of Dr. Zajc from a distant town. I would have returned to the Slandrova Brigade except that Dr. Zajc was killed by the Germans the next day, and I had no choice but to stay. Both of the wounded airmen were in need of glucose shots. Although we had obtained some medicine from the nearby town of Kamnik, the one with the most serious injury needed much more. Together with our wounded, the Americans were sent to our new hospital in Kamniška Bela.

The condition of the two least wounded improved daily. After ten days at the hospital they were completely recovered, volunteering to help at the hospital and even splitting wood. But we couldn't do any more for the airman with the spinal fracture. Every evening he read chapters from the Bible to the other two airmen. He removed his rings and watch and requested that they be given to his wife since "there is no hope for me anyway." The captain was buried at the hospital and his two fellow airmen left for a long and dangerous journey to Bela Krajina.

* * * * *

Dr. Domitrovič appeared deeply touched as he reminisced. I showed him the list of the airmen rescued by the Slovene Partisans, and he was greatly relieved when he found the names of his two patients, knowing now that they had safely returned to America.

The director of the Kamnik museum, Zora Torkar, provided some supporting documentation from the Institute for Workers Movement, Ljubljana:

It is requested that the Head of the Anglo-American mission, Captain Saggers, be informed of the following:
On July 20, 1944, an Allied airman died in one of the Kamnik posts. The information obtained from OK KPS states:

Personal data: Lieutenant Otto H. Hinds, 0-15-392, pilot, born 14.X.17.

Address: 9th Street, Boulder, Colorado.

Cause of Death: Fractura vertebrae, fractura complicata femori, fractura fibulae sin., astenia gravis et decubitus.

Because of his strong physique and the intensive treatment received while at the hospital, the pilot survived for two months before he died. He is buried in the close vicinity of the hospital.

The burial took place on 21 July 1944 at 17:00 in the presence of the hospital personnel and the manager of the post. The ceremony was executed without the presence of a priest and was conducted in our language (Slovene). The grave was decorated with our mountain flowers and greenery, and a wooden cross was put on his grave. A bottle containing the deceased's statistics was buried next to the cross.

We do not possess any other data.

The head staff, major [signature illegible]

Medical Superintendent, Capt.

Dr. Peter Drzaj

Date: 3 September 1944

On the day that the airmen descended in Slovenia, May 29, 1944, Janko Urbanc (Partisan name: "Olga"), a member of the Kamnik Department Committee, was responsible for the interaction between the courier service and the army and was engaged in his business in the Moravska valley. While observing the action of the warplanes in the sky, he saw a heavy bomber crash not far from where he stood. He mounted his horse and took a shortcut to the scene of the disaster. He recounted his participation in the event:

* * * * *

I don't remember if it was the Sunday or Monday after Ascension Day [it was Monday]. A heavy bomber approached from the direction of Limbarska Gora flying towards Velika Planina. It was obvious that something was wrong with the aircraft, for a few seconds later it crashed into the mountain.

I was directed to respond immediately. My first responsibility was to reach the airmen before the Germans posted in the nearby towns and villages arrived. I was joined by Jože Pirš ("Luka"), who was in charge of the Partisan hospital Kolovec, in case there were any wounded that required hospitalization.

We soon arrived at the crash site and found that Partisan couriers were the first ones there. We were struck by the horror of the scene — two of the crew

Herdsmen and Partisans at the funeral of an American airman buried at Velika Planina on May 29, 1944. Photo taken by Janko Urbanc ("Olga").

were dead and one was seriously injured. The injured airman was taken to the closest hospital, Kamniška Bela. The two deceased were buried at the site. We conducted the burial with as much respect and solemnity as possible under the circumstances. I made a speech, mentioning the Allied effort fighting against the Nazi occupation and the help being offered by the Allied forces risking their own lives for our mutual cause. I also took some pictures on that occasion.

I wondered what had happened to the rest of the crew. They could have hidden in one of the numerous haylofts in the surrounding countryside.

I returned about a month later and was informed by herdsmen that they found a stranger in uniform by one of the nearby haylofts. Although he may have had some nourishment with him when he jumped, it was remarkable that he could sustain himself without proper food and stay in hiding for so long a period of time. The herdsmen first noticed him as he drank rainwater from a hole he had dug in the ground in front of the hayloft. He was so exhausted that they took him to a Partisan hospital.

On the way to the hospital we stopped at Primož's house. On the table was a loaf of bread. We had to physically restrain him from grabbing it and eating it, for we knew that his digestive system couldn't handle too much food at one time. The remainder of the journey was very difficult and demanded caution. Later I heard that after a period of care at the hospital, he had fully recovered and was escorted on the long march to the Partisan airstrip in Bela Krajina.

The rescued airmen were very grateful. They informed us that they would all probably get leave when they returned to their base, but afterwards they would continue flying in combat. They also promised to circle over the mountain to let us know that they had returned safely to their base. It so happened that an airplane did indeed circle over the mountain later on.

One of the airmen parachuted near the town of Kamnik. The Germans rushed to capture him, leaving their car in the valley before climbing up the mountain. By the time they reached the landing place, all that remained was the airman's parachute, for the Partisans had arrived earlier and rescued him. While the Germans searched for the American, the Partisans burned the car. Witnessing the car burning from afar, the Germans began shooting at the Partisans and, in revenge, burned the nearby homesteads after evicting the inhabitants.

I also learned that three of the crew members had parachuted somewhere in the Tuhinjska valley and were captured by the Germans.

I wrote all of the addresses of the dead, wounded, and rescued airmen in my notebook, but it was lost during the last German offensive just before the end of the war.

* * * * *

George Bertuzzi, who successfully bailed out of a burning bomber and landed in the vicinity of the village Vir.

However, Urbanc did preserve the extraordinary photographs that document the contributions of the Slovene Partisans.

Both Zora Torkar and Mirina Zupančič, also from Kamnik, made inquiries after the war on the fate of the airmen. Zora actually corresponded with one of the crew members, George Bertuzzi from Connecticut.

Years later, without previously hinting that he might visit shortly, George arrived in Slovenia. He had been captured and did not know what had happened to the other members of the crew. While discussing the events of 1944 he recalled only a few details, such as a brook and a hill beside some house, perhaps a mill. Mirina provided some background information but not enough to help total recall. Bertuzzi returned to America and wrote Mirina with additional background:

> I will try to give you as much information as possible about the flight you are interested in. I do not know the names of all of the men that were aboard the plane because I was flying as a substitute Radio-gunner that day.
>
> We left Cerignola that day of May 29, 1944 to bomb targets at Wollersdorf, Austria. While flying over Yugoslavia the plane caught fire and had to be abandoned. The plane was a B-17 Flying Fortress from the 301st Bomb Group, 353 Bomb Squadron. The pilot's name was Frank Didemizia from Beacon, New York. I believe the ball turret gunner was M. Sorenson from Waltham, Mass. I do not recall any of the names of the rest of the crew. I have been trying to contact the pilot but have been unsuccessfull [*sic*] so far. If I am able to obtain more information I will write to you again. When I returned home I was informed that the copilot had died in a hospital in Yugoslavia. I believe the Ball Turret Gunner went down in the plane and was killed. Could you supply me with the name of the soldier that is buried in the grave in the pictures you sent to me?
>
> The Air Force notified my parents that the airplane went down in the area of Celje and that eight parachutes were observed. There were ten men aboard so that accounts for the copilot having trouble with his parachute and the Ball Turret Gunner going down in the plane. The pilot and I met on the ground. I don't know the name of the town. I landed on a mountain side along a river. I thought the name of the town began with [K]. I went to Kamnik when I was in Yugoslavia in 1985, The copilot and I were captured at a home close to the river. There were three or four young girls there and they were attending to our injuries when the Germans captured us. We were taken to a prison not far from where we were captured and

put into solitary confinement until the 4th of July and then moved to a P.O.W. camp in Gross Tychow, Germany. If I could locate the prison and the people that helped me I would like to return to Yugoslavia again. The prison was an old one built years ago and I assumed for hardened criminals. The rooms were small with thick cement walls, barred windows and no modern plumbing. The Germans were using it for their headquarters. Also young girls would walk around the courtyard at night and sing songs. They were guarded by German soldiers. How can I locate the prison? There can be but one in that area. I hope to return to Yugoslavia one day and meet you.

Sincerely,
George Bertuzzi

Although the circumstances of the tragedy that befell the crew of the American aircraft that crashed on May 29, 1944, in the foothills of Mala and Velika Planina were partially explained, all of the facts surrounding that event will probably never be uncovered.

Chapter 8

A Grateful Patient

Among the many contacts that Floridian John Hribar made with airmen downed in Yugoslavia during World War II was Herman Lipkin, who also lived in Florida. Lipkin provided the following recollections of his experience with the Partisans in a 1979 letter.

We were based near Foggia, Italy and part of the 15th Air Force. Our plane was hit by anti-aircraft over our target and we could not keep up with our formation. We were then attacked by German fighters. In the battle I was severely wounded in the face and leg. The plane started to smoke. The bottom hatch was opened and I was thrown out by one of our crew and I opened my parachute. I looked up and could see that the plane was still flying but losing altitude. I now remember coming down and landing in a tree in an area that looked like a forest. I do not know how long I was there before some people came, cut me down from the tree and took me to their village. I was bandaged and soon taken to the hospital in the mountains. The trip must have taken three or four days.

At the hospital I met a few other Americans, but none was as seriously wounded as I was. I was in the hospital about a week and had not been operated on when another crewman, named Palmer Lerun, who recently had his leg amputated, was put in the bed alongside of me. It appeared that he went into shock, for he ranted and raved for days. One night he appeared perfectly rational and his mind normal as he shook me and asked how long we were there. He suddenly stiffened and was quiet. I knew that he had died, and I lay there all night thinking that I was going to be next. It was 3 a.m.

Herman Lipkin, on crutches, in the Rog forest after his leg amputation.

when they arrived to check on Lerun and found him dead. He was buried in Slovenia.

The doctor then explained to me that they would have to cut off my leg and they waited for a well-respected surgeon to come and do the job. He must have done a good job because I am still living and, although I suffer from various pains, I am still thankful to be in this world. To this day I don't know why I survived and Lerun didn't. There was very little medicine, no blood transfusions, and even the bandages were boiled and used over again.

After four months I was awakened in the middle of the night and advised that I would be leaving. After a tearful farewell, I was placed on a stretcher and carried by two Partisans with two others accompanying us as guards. During the journey the guards and the stretcher bearers swapped roles every couple of hours. At the end of a day long trip we arrived at a small village where two trucks powered by wood-burning engines awaited us in the village square. I sat in the front next to the driver with the back of the truck filled with rifle-toting Partisans. The second truck was also filled with Partisans. I don't remember how long or how far we traveled but recall that the roads were in terrible shape.

We finally arrived at a town where, after a few hours [of] rest, the sound of approaching airplane engines indicated that an airstrip was nearby. Shortly thereafter, two men carried me on the stretcher to the edge of a runway where barrels of oil and arms were being unloaded from the aircraft. When the unloading was completed, one of the Partisans requested the British pilot to take me on board on the return flight back to Italy. I finally prevailed after some argumentative discussion that centered around the pilot not having any orders to evacuate anyone. Once in the air the British crew radioed ahead for an American ambulance to meet us when we landed.

After an operation on my face and a month's recuperation, I was finally shipped back to the U.S. where I underwent additional surgery on my leg before being discharged from the service a year later.

I would now like to thank all the good people who tried their best to save my life. From the pictures you sent me I now remember the doctors. Peter and Maria and a Russian girl called Tamara. If the doctor is ever found and if he remembers me, I think that he might recall that I gave him my watch before I left.

Getting the pictures brought back a lot of memories. Although it was 35 years ago, I can see things as if it was yesterday.

Partisan airstrip during the period when wounded Partisans and airmen were brought there by horse and wagon.

Lipkin's first letter was written 35 years after his stay in Slovenia. The photographs that he mentioned were taken by Dr. Janez Milčinski, code-named "Peter," at the Partisan hospital where Lipkin was being treated. Dr. Milčinski is now president of the Academy of Science and Arts in Ljubljana.

Milčinski remembers the event quite well. He was watching how the door of the plane fell to the ground first, and then he saw the airmen bail out. After the wounded Lipkin was taken to a hospital, it was determined that his wounds were serious. The bones in his knee were smashed. It was necessary to amputate his leg, and the operation was successfully performed by Dr. Bogdan Brecelj, who was the late President Tito's doctor. As far as Dr. Milčinski remembers, there were a few more American airmen at the hospital at that time. One of them — Lerun, who was mentioned by Lipkin — died, but the others were not seriously injured.

Dr. Marija Jeras, who assisted with the operation, remembered the night when Herman Lipkin was brought to the hospital.

> This American patient was given all the necessary treatment given to everyone who came to our hospital — of course, everything was provided that we had access to in those hard times. Antiaircraft shell metal fragments injured his face and also caused serious wounds in his left leg. When Lipkin recovered after the shock, we explained to him that there was no other choice but to amputate his leg. His pains were getting worse and worse, and I remember Lipkin himself asking us one night to operate on his leg because he could not stand the pains any longer.

A medical file that is kept in the Museum of the People's Movement states that Lipkin's operation was performed on May 2, 1944, by Dr. Bogdan Brecelj, assisted by nurse Marija Jeras and Dr. Janez Milčinski.

Dr. Jeras continued her recollections:

> I also remember another very young wounded airman, Palmer Lerun. Unfortunately, complications arose, and he died. While one other American crewman on the plane [Warren Stuckey] was only slightly wounded and left the hospital soon afterwards, Herman Lipkin stayed with us for at least four months. During this period we had to move him and our other patients to various underground posts that were being readied in the event of a sudden enemy breakthrough. As far as I remember, Lipkin was a calm and undemanding patient. Perhaps the only Slovene words that he learned were "*močnik ni dobro* (cornmeal no good)."
>
> It seems to me even now he isn't aware of the unusual circum-

stances connected with his treatment. His eyes were bandaged —
as were all others that were transported to our hospital — so that he
didn't have any idea as to the location of his stay nor of the villages
and enemy posts en route to the hospital. In this way no one could
betray the hospital location in case they were captured and tor-
tured. Lipkin did not know that we were constantly surrounded by
the enemy and in mortal danger if discovered. We Partisans knew
about one tragedy that occurred when the enemy, during an
Autumn 1943 offensive, discovered the hospital at Pugled and
massacred all of the 21 wounded Partisans.

Dr. Jeras requested that I relate her memories to Herman Lipkin and let him
know that the staff had pleasant memories of him and wished him well.

I received a letter from Herman Lipkin in October of 1988 in which he
wrote:

> I am now 66 years old and although I thought of visiting
> Yugoslavia years ago, it is not virtually possible for me to make
> such a long trip. I spend most of my days on crutches and cannot
> wear my prosthesis for too long a period of time and suffer with
> backaches and pain in my hips.
>
> . . . My wife would like me to write an autobiography about the
> events of my army life and how after so many years I got in touch
> with the people who helped me recover from my wounds. It would
> make for interesting reading, but . . .

Chapter 9

The Longest Mission

by John C. Rucigay

Wasp's Nest

It started as a typical bombing mission into occupied Europe on July 19, 1944, with the participants from the 464th Heavy Bombardment Group based in southern Italy, near Cerignola. Little did we realize that one of the statements at the early morning briefing would play an important role later that day: "There are reports of Partisan activity in the Istrian Peninsula should any of you be forced to land there and seek assistance."

We had arisen at 4:30 a.m. and had our usual breakfast of powdered eggs and a canteen of strong black coffee. Entering the briefing tent with the rest of the crews, we learned that the selected target for the day was the Allach Aircraft Engine factory in Munich, Germany. This would be the first time that we would bomb the German homeland, and we looked forward to it with some trepidation. The usual information on flight routes, target landmarks, and antiaircraft and fighter strength, in addition to weather en route and at the target site, was provided before we finally synchronized our watches. It was 5:30 a.m.

In addition to me as the copilot, our crew consisted of pilot Tom Mac-Donald, bombardier Bob Denison, navigator Joe Lidiak, flight engineer Bob Garin, radioman Guy Howard, nose turret gunner Bob Marcum, top turret gunner Merle Weik, ball turret gunner Charles Cartmille, and tail turret gunner John Lewis.

We noted where in the 39-ship formation our four-engined bomber was scheduled, since this determined the risk from enemy fighters and, for the pilots, indicated the degree of work required to fly formation to and from the target. We were assigned to fly wing — one side of a three-plane *V* — in the

John Rucigay (front, second from left) and crew of *Little One*.

second *V* of one of the forward "boxes." At least we were not the last aircraft in the box.

The flight formation for the group consisted of two *V*-shaped echelons of three boxes each. Each box in the forward echelon consisted of seven aircraft: a *V* of three followed by a diamond of four aircraft. The Group Command pilot flew in the lead plane, with the right box slightly higher and behind and the left box slightly lower and behind. The second echelon was situated behind and below the first echelon. It was similar to the first formation except that each box consisted of only six planes, the diamond of four being replaced by a *V* of three aircraft.

We all received our parachutes and escape kits, which consisted of $42 in U.S. currency, bouillon soup cubes, matches, needle and thread, compass, and maps of southern France, northern Italy, and Yugoslavia, made of waterproof silk.

After a ground inspection of our aircraft (*Little One*) and crew equipment, the engines were started. We taxied into the line of B-24 Liberators and proceeded toward the twin steel-matted runways that ran parallel with the valley. Takeoffs were timed at 20-second intervals on alternate runways (or 40 seconds behind the previous B-24 on that runway).

Each box leader delayed his first turn after takeoff so that the last aircraft would be in position immediately after leaving the field boundary and turning 180 degrees. It required only a few more climbing turns before the entire Group was loosely assembled over the Adriatic Sea. Contact with the remainder of the 15th Air Force was established at rendezvous points over the Adriatic, after which the entire Air Force proceeded through the friendly skies over the sea, climbing all the while to the target area.

Troubles Begin

Trouble started before we reached Munich. The navigator had gotten a new "G" box (radar navigation equipment), and a fire started in this unit as we neared the halfway point to the target. Although it was eventually extinguished, it seemed to precipitate our troubles. Shortly thereafter, the propeller on the number 1 engine "ran away" and had to be feathered. We could maintain an altitude of only 16,000 feet while the rest of the Group continued climbing to 22,000 feet. However, we managed to maintain our relationship with the Group, albeit 6,000 feet below them, thus arriving together at the IP — the initial point, or starting point, of a bomb run.

Bombs were released after selecting another target in Munich. Flak was heavy and *Little One* received a few scratches, as did the crew. We made a left turn and headed for home, independent of the Group.

Eventually, the number 2 engine failed as a result of the flak, as did the electrical system. Consequently, we had no electrical supply for the power-

Anton Levak, from Pula, was repeatedly lucky. As a Partisan from an Istrian detachment, he convoyed Allies from Krnica to Partisan outposts near St. Katarina.

operated turrets, radio, intercommunication, or instruments except for the airspeed indicator, altimeter, "needle and ball," and magnetic compass (which was not reliable since level flight could not be maintained due to the asymmetric engine thrust).

As we headed the aircraft back through the Alps at 16,000 feet, the number 2 engine kept windmilling, thus creating additional drag. Heading for a pass, we noticed a formation of German fighter planes coming directly toward us. Luckily they were intercepted by American fighters, and in the ensuing dogfight the Germans were scattered. We continued south for another hour, our only defense the two .50-caliber machine guns mounted at the rear waist windows. Eventually reaching northern Italy and not knowing exactly where we were, we aimed on a course that, unbeknownst to us, would take us over Udine, Italy.

Luckily, another American fighter, a P-51 Mustang aircraft, realizing our plight, purposely flew over the city and attracted flak. After seeing the flak, we bypassed the city, going out over the Adriatic. Another P-51 came alongside and flew off of our right wing. We communicated with the pilot by sign language and indicated by pointing to our earphones that our radio was inoperative. He recorded our Group markings and departed. (Unfortunately, this information was never transmitted to our Bomb Group or documented in the Group's records.)

We continued south and lost the number 3 engine as we approached Pola, Italy (now Pula, Yugoslavia). We then had a single-engine bomber that could not maintain altitude. The shoreline was close by, and we let the remaining number 4 engine drive the aircraft back toward the Istrian Peninsula.

We started at approximately 15,000 feet, and the plane was descending at a rate of 500 feet per minute. We knew we had to bail out. The pilot, radio operator, nose gunner, navigator, and I left the airplane via the front bomb bay; the bombardier, tail gunner, flight engineer, ball gunner, and top turret gunner parachuted from the tail escape hatch. On my way out I noticed that the navigator had left his watch on the radio table. I picked it up and put it in my coverall pocket. Then, at an altitude of 7,000 feet, I saw a cloud pass under the plane and decided to jump immediately. We had previously been schooled to count to ten before pulling the parachute rip cord, but I never reached seven. The chute opened with a snap, and I saw the plane leaving me about 100 yards away. I don't recall seeing the pilot bail out, but I watched the plane as it made a gradual turn to the right, giving me an eerie feeling. I was not prepared for the aircraft to contact the ground when it did, since I thought it was a few thousand feet above the earth. But a ball of flame enveloped the aircraft as it slid along the ground for a few hundred yards.

Where is Denny, the Bombardier?

It appeared as if I had been nailed to the sky. I wasn't conscious of any rate of descent, so, to keep from getting bored, I decided to experiment with possible emergency maneuvers. We had been taught in school that if you grab one of the two parachute harness vertical risers, you can spill the air from the chute to one side and thus control the direction of fall. Upon pulling the riser, however, violent oscillations occurred, and I did no more experimenting. About halfway through the descent, the harness started to cut into my groin, so to relieve the pressure I had to pull myself upward on both risers.

The thrill of a parachute jump cannot be duplicated. The silence is unearthly. Only during the last thousand feet of descent did I notice any downward sensation. When I got within a few hundred feet of the ground, I looked down and saw that one of the crew was directly below me. I shouted to him; he looked up and waved. It was Merle Weik, the top turret gunner. I figured it would take me another minute or more to touch the ground, but just as I looked downward a second time, the ground "came up" and caused my knee to hit my chin before I rolled over. Fortunately, I was completely relaxed at this point and suffered no further injury.

It was a nice afternoon, and we congratulated one another as we were taking off our parachutes and looking for some place to bury them. Although the surrounding terrain was quite hilly, we had luckily landed in a soft, plowed field. We looked up and noticed that one of our casual observers was a tall, dark gent waving a big "horse pistol." We told him, "We are *Amerikanski!*," whereupon he motioned for us to follow him.

We walked along a country road — actually two ruts — for a few hundred yards and then down a path through a wooded area. Within 15 minutes we heard the engines of an aircraft, and our guide motioned for us to hide in the brush. Glancing up, we saw a tri-motored Italian Breda bomber skimming over the countryside about 100 yards above the ground, apparently searching for survivors. It disappeared after one or two more passes.

After walking 20 minutes, Merle and I and our escort came to a barn-like structure, which we entered. Amidst the bare surroundings was a rough-hewn table, behind which were seated two dark figures, obviously the hosts. They tried to make us feel at home, and all three of them persuaded us to sit down and relax.

It was about 2:00 p.m. when we lit our first cigarettes and passed the pack to the others. Sensing we might be hungry, our hosts brought out two bowls of quite tasty chicory coffee and some black bread. Our man with the "horse pistol" then informed us that we were among Partisans.

It was then that we experienced our first adventure with Yugoslav flies. We were scooping them out of the coffee between sips. I almost stopped drinking after I pulled a "winged raisin" from between my teeth.

A half-hour after our arrival, we were beckoned toward the door and followed two of the guides for about 45 minutes before we came upon a camp in the woods. During the course of the next few hours, six of the members of our crew trickled in. As the parachutes were of no use to us, we gave them to our hosts. They indicated that they did not necessarily want them, as anyone caught with a parachute or part of one was immediately suspect. I therefore took the pilot chute (a small one-foot-diameter miniature chute that initially springs from the pack and pulls the rest of the parachute out as the air fills it) and some of the nylon panels for possible future use.

At sunset there were eight of us. Two of the crew members — the pilot, Tom MacDonald, and the bombardier, Bob Denison — were missing from our group. The rest of us were in pretty fair condition with the exception of a few superficial flak wounds and the radio operator's sprained ankle.

We sat around the camp until about 8:00 p.m. when our escort rounded us up and motioned for us to follow. Within half an hour we came upon a small, pleasant hamlet: Krnica. The whole population thronged around us as if we were a wonder, but our guide seemed aloof to all the ruckus and continued herding us to a spacious house. While the Yugoslavs talked excitedly among themselves, we occupied ourselves by picking out the pretty girls in the crowd. Someone beckoned us to enter the house. It was dark by then, and in the lamplight we distinguished two rooms, bare except for a long table at the end of them. They indicated that we should seat ourselves around this table as

Meeting at Krnica, near where the airmen landed.

wine, bread, and large bowls of lettuce were brought in. After the entree we braced ourselves for a large meal, but it turned out that we had had it — that was the end of the meal.

The townspeople trooped into the house to gape at us. With full glasses in front of us, we became more and more at ease. Finally, someone brought in an accordion, and soon we were dancing and making merry. A few hours previous, above Munich, we could not have dreamt that this would be happening. I myself took the accordion in my hands and played some folk music. Meanwhile, Merle Weik was pinching derrieres.

About midnight, someone made a speech. We were ready for the sack, having been up since 5:00 a.m. When someone motioned for us to leave the building, we eagerly looked forward to sleep. Each of us was thinking where he would rest his tired bones as our hosts motioned for us to follow them outside. We noticed someone leading a donkey, and it was indicated that our radioman, Guy Howard, who had sprained his ankle while landing, should ride it. This should have alerted us, but little did we then realize that we were embarking on an eight-hour stroll.

That first night we initially headed south, and during the course of the march we stuck to back trails. At one point we saw aerial flares and heard exploding bombs and antiaircraft gunfire in the distance, thus obtaining a

Partisans on a typical endless march.

directional "fix" since we knew that the British were bombing Pola. This raid occurred around two or three in the morning.

We always walked in single file with a guide at the head of the column and one at the rear along the cart track. From time to time a "*Stoj* (Stop)!" rang out, and we all had to stand still while the lead guide identified himself to a Partisan.

We continued walking, cursing at the rough stones in the path. Eventually, about an hour or so after sunrise, we heard our last "*Stoj!*" and entered a small clearing in the woods that served as a Partisan camp. We washed up, gratefully plopped down on some blankets on the ground, and in no time at all fell asleep.

The next day we met the pilot, Tom MacDonald. He had been the last to leave the aircraft and had apparently drifted farther away from us. Now there were nine of us of the original ten; only Bob Denison, the bombardier, was still missing.

The events of that day and evening set the pattern for the next few weeks: Walk the back trails at night for at least eight hours, and sleep during the daylight hours. Sleeping was always fulfilled in a wooded area, either outdoors or inside a lean-to. I still recall being pinched by the loose boards of the second level used for our bed in one lean-to. Fortunately we were blessed with good weather, and at least everything was dry.

We were bivouacked in a wooded area on the third or fourth day after our landing and had an opportunity to wash ourselves and our clothing, using the water quite liberally. We drastically reduced this health habit upon discovering that all the water used for drinking and sanitation was obtained "under fire," that is, the Partisans literally had to fight for the water by retrieving it from the enemy-held territory.

It was during this period that we exchanged some gifts with the Partisans. We left our Colt .45 pistols with them before leaving Yugoslavia, and they in turn gave each of us a Partisan cap made of heavy felt, navy blue in color with a red star at the peak in front. I still have mine.

A few days later as we skirted a ridge, we came to a road leading to a small hamlet. The road was lined with shrubbery and small trees on both sides. It ran for about 100 yards before meeting with the first building, which was a barn on the left-hand side. We had been walking all night, and since dawn was about an hour away, our guide informed us by gestures that we were to sleep in this barn. We entered, finding our way by the moonlight up the ramp through the double doors. Being pretty well exhausted and having anticipated our rest for the past hour, we quickly made beds for ourselves on the straw-covered floor to the left of the door. The right side of the barn was occupied by another group of men whose presence was made known by their snoring and heavy breathing.

Some time later, shortly after the sun had risen, there was a commotion at the other end of the barn that awakened me. I noticed that the group with which we had shared our lodging was being herded outside. There must have been a dozen of them, and it was only then that I realized that we had been sharing quarters with some captured German soldiers! They were an elderly group in their forties and fifties, men who moved slowly with a resigned air. Later on during the course of the day we learned that these captured men were reservists who had been pressed into military service to relieve younger troops for front-line duty.

I went back to sleep and woke up around 11:00 a.m. Leaving the barn, I started to take stock of the countryside that heretofore had been shrouded in darkness. It seemed that we were on a slope of a hill that overlooked a broad plain through which meandered a creek. The thought occurred to us immediately that we should take advantage of the stream and wash both our bodies and our clothes. Having eaten, Bob Garin, Guy Howard, and I proceeded down the road to the bottom of the hill and then struck out directly toward the creek (the Partisans permitted only three of us to go to the stream at one time; any more would have caused too great an attraction). It was a matter of minutes before we were standing on the bank looking down about five feet into a foot or so of water that babbled in the center of the stream bed. We jumped down and immediately started undressing, eager for our first bath.

We washed our clothes, and after spreading them out over the warm rocks to dry, we splashed around the water, using friction for soap. Half-exhausted, we sunned ourselves until our clothes were dried. While we were sitting around in our underwear, I proceeded to mend the remnants of my socks and underwear using the needle and thread that had so thoughtfully been provided by the Army Air Forces in our GI escape kits.

A Hot-Tempered Girl

I happened to glance up and saw a girl of about 16 walk toward us with her hands thrust in the pockets of her skirt.

"*Dober dan* (Good day)," she greeted us.

I answered her greeting in her language, after which she inquired what we were doing. I replied that we were washing.

"Are there more of you?" she asked seriously, to which I replied, "*Ne* (No)."

Howard kept interrupting with, "What did she say?" The conversation was rapidly getting out of hand, for I felt that my acquaintance with the Croatian language at that point had been all but spent. I wanted to convey to her that we could not continue the conversation because of the language barrier, so I blurted out, "*Amerikanski!*" At that, her face broke into a broad smile, and she informed us that her first thought was that we were Germans, since my two companions were blond. Withdrawing her hands from her pockets, she showed us a small Italian Beretta automatic pistol neatly palmed in her right hand. She explained she would not have hesitated to shoot us if circumstances had so dictated.

It was about this time that the question of food assumed a paramount position in the majority of our discussions. Until this time we had been eating the simple fare of the Partisans, but we now yearned for a meal with some seasoning. The diet of the Partisans, albeit varied, suffered from a lack of condiments, the most important of which was salt. For food, the Partisans depended partly on the goodwill of the local inhabitants but to a greater extent on what they could glean from raids on German supply bases and anti-Partisan sources of supply. There was a certain amount of requisitioning done from the local populace for which the donor received credit.

It was the custom of the Partisans that any young livestock that they captured would be traded to any sympathetic farmer who wanted to replace his old livestock. This was evident when our meals included beef; the flavor and texture left much to be desired, for it was tough and stringy.

The sparse evening meal having been eaten, we would sit around the camp conjuring up visions of thick steaks smothered in mushrooms and onions, veal cutlets, roast beef with mashed potatoes and natural gravy — and on and on. We became quite interested in local cooking customs and watched the baking of black bread. The dough was placed on a flat steel plate that doubled as a stove top. The wood coals were then removed from underneath the plate and heaped over the mound of dough. After a couple of hours, a loaf of brown bread emerged. The size had not appreciably increased due to the lack of yeast, and the shape and weight approximated that of a brick.

The Partisan cook, George, was good-natured and affable and almost always wore a smile on his face. On one occasion he produced a rare treat, a jar of strawberry jam, which he immediately spread over some thick slices of bread and handed to us.

Early one evening a Partisan, armed to the teeth and then some, rode into our area on horseback. He had a bandolier of ammunition slung across one shoulder, a rifle on his back, a brace of pistols on his hips, and hand grenades suspended from almost every part of his torso. His mount, a substantial-looking bay, appeared as eager as his rider. Our curiosity was much aroused by the sight of this lone horseman, as a mounted man was a rare sight in this type of countryside. We inquired why he was so heavily armed and were informed to our amazement that he was bound for the railroad marshalling yard in Fiume, Italy (Rijeka, Yugoslavia), where he intended to conduct a one-man raid. It was his intent to break into one of the boxcars and make off with as much booty as his horse could possibly carry.

One day, Joe Lidiak, John Lewis, Bob Garin, and myself — all Catholics — saw a small church about 1,500 yards distant and decided to take a walk over to it. It was a hot, sunny day, and the exercise brought beads of sweat to our brows.

When we came near the building, nestled in a stand of massive trees atop a small hillock, we perceived that the church was a chapel. We welcomed the cool, quiet shade that greeted us as we entered the quaint old edifice. We knelt down and said a prayer. This was my first visit to a church in over two weeks, since I missed Mass the Sunday before the unlucky mission.

The priest, a short, slim, youngish-looking man, had come outside to welcome us. We exchanged greetings and thereafter carried on an animated conversation using his limited knowledge of English and whatever linguistic tools we had at our disposal. We gleaned that the Partisans had little to do with the clergy but allowed them to come and go unhindered among the communicants.

During the beginning of our three-day sojourn in this small hill hamlet we met Joco, whom we called "Joe." Joe was a native in his late fifties, of medium height, grizzled features, and nondescript clothing. He was to act as our interpreter. Joe had once been to the United States prior to World War I, and this visit earned him a certain status among his countrymen. However, his proficiency in English was about as limited as our knowledge of Croatian. Furthermore, his recollections of Americana dated back to five-cent beers, free lunches, and wooden cigar store Indians. Joe's stock-in-trade reply to any conversational gambit on our part, whether question, statement, or casual remark, was, "Yes."

After we became aware that he didn't understand nine-tenths of our conversation, we purposely posed him "loaded" questions knowing full well that his answer would be to the affirmative. His answer of "Yes" would provoke spasms of laughter on our part and his.

It was on the third day of our stay that, Bob Denison, "Denny," the bombardier, arrived. Although he looked rather exhausted, he proceeded to tell us his long story.

Denny was the first to jump from the aft escape hatch, soon after we crossed the coastline. He remembered that if he would delay opening his parachute until he was very close to the ground, it would minimize his chances of detection by enemy troops. In retrospect, considering that it was his first jump, he did an admirable job of escaping notice. Indeed, he fell over 10,000 feet before he pulled the rip cord. The ensuing jolt caused by popping the chute set up a pendulum motion; he touched ground on the third swing and sprained both ankles. He landed in a wooded area and realized upon hearing German being spoken that he was only 50 yards from a German antiaircraft gun crew. As he couldn't walk and there was still the possibility of capture by the Germans, he crawled, dragging all of his equipment to some dense shrubbery where he spent the next few days recuperating.

His first thought was to get back to Allied territory, so he started walking along the shore looking for some means of transport across the Adriatic. He soon came across a rowboat, which he commandeered. He set out for the western shore, but after a few hours of rowing he found himself beached back near where he had started from. Deciding that the water route was not feasible, he determined to try something else. He walked south, following the coastline, and presently came to the city of Pola.

It was about eight o'clock in the morning, and it was obvious that the German troops had just had breakfast, for Denny saw them swinging the mess kits as they walked by him. The Germans paid no attention to him since he wore a nondescript outfit consisting of khaki pants and a sweatshirt. His black "butch" haircut and boyish appearance could easily have passed him off as a young Italian on his way to work.

About this time he spotted a bicycle parked at the opposite curb. He started to cross the street to steal it, but the owner beat him to it, and he was never suspected. He continued strolling through the city observing many fuel depots, radar installations, gun emplacements, and the like, information he eventually passed on to Allied Intelligence.

Before he knew it, he found himself on the outskirts of the city on a main road heading into the countryside. A German sentry stationed in his cubicle observed his approach and departure but said nothing. Denny turned around once and noticed the guard studying his shoes. Playing it cool, he continued walking.

After existing for five days on berries and water plus one meal from a peasant household, he was getting desperate. He finally accosted a peasant woman and blurted out that he was an American and wanted help. She ran away from him. It wasn't long afterward that Denny heard a shout behind him. Turning around, he saw a trio of rugged-looking peasants making threatening gestures at him. His immediate reaction was that these men were quisling guerrillas — traitors who collaborated with the invading enemy — so he bolted. He ran up a long hill, the three men in hot pursuit. The chase ended when one of them tackled him. All four sat down to catch their breath. The trio turned out to be local Partisans who had been alerted to his presence by the peasant woman. A few days later we heard Denny's story first-hand when he joined us. It had been a full week since we had last seen him.

We wondered what had happened to our aircraft and what action the Germans had taken after inspecting the wreckage. Early one evening after finishing supper, we were given some Charm candies, which were a welcome relief from the usual soup made from flour with chunks of old beef thrown in. We wondered from where the candies had come and were then told the full story of the events following the crash.

The Partisans had surrounded the whole area containing the wreckage,

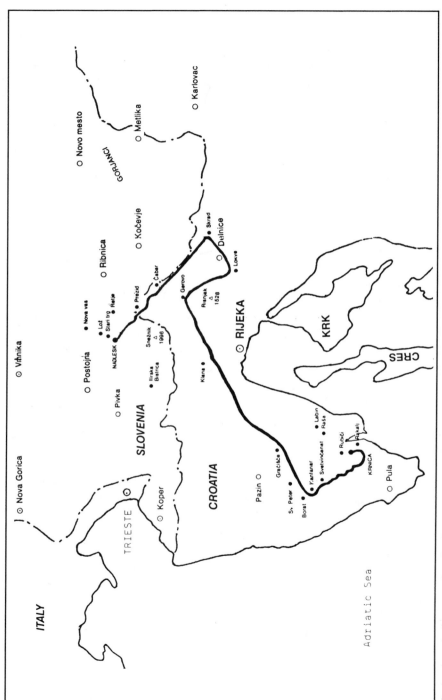

Rucigay's route, from parachute landing to the airstrip at Nadlesk.

concealing themselves. The Germans knew of the crash and its location and had sent a patrol to examine the remains. They walked into a perfect ambush and were wiped out to a man. This was the usual method employed by the Partisans to replenish their supplies; they stripped the Germans of everything they had — even the tires were used to re-sole their shoes.

Only after the skirmish was over did the Partisans inspect the wreckage. The free-swivel machine guns normally mounted in the waist had been thrown clear as had the life raft, which is normally stowed above the wing. One of the .50-caliber guns was undamaged, and the Partisans used it as a light cannon; the other gun had a bent barrel and was used for spare parts. The Charm candies we enjoyed that evening were part of a survival kit included with the life raft.

The next evening as we sat around the fireplace where the Partisans cooked, one of them proceeded to stir-fry chunks of beef in a large pan. By the aroma steaming from the saucepan, this particular evening meal promised to be the best since we had parachuted. Portions consisting of small chunks of beef in a greasy gravy were given to each of us. It was delicious and we quickly ate everything, sopping up the gravy with pieces of bread. Later, a bottle of slivovitz — plum brandy — appeared, and each of us took a mouthful. It burned our throats on the way down to our stomachs, but it tasted very good. On the few occasions that I drank slivovitz in later years, it never tasted as good as the drink we had had that evening. The next morning, each of us experienced diarrhea; was it the richness, the grease, or the slivovitz? I concluded that our systems were not used to the fat in·the stew and relished once again the thought of the good meal we had had the previous evening.

Each one of us had a history of gas problems since we landed in Yugoslavia due to the change in diet, exercise, and the like, and consequently there was much flatulence while we walked in single file, causing unpleasant odors to waft through the column behind the offender. We finally made a rule: Anyone passing wind would have to step out of line to the side of the column in order to show mercy on those behind. The degree of gas accumulation was soon obvious — someone was always walking alongside of the column!

We had been wearing the same cotton underwear for a week without any opportunity to wash it. Consequently, the dirt and sweat stiffened the cloth, with the end result being that the material appeared to crack instead of tear. In addition, the stitches were unraveling. Even so, it was better than not having any underwear. But our experience with the diarrhea soon resolved the issue, and we threw our underpants away.

As we walked near the old Italian/Yugoslav border, we noticed that some of the roads were in very poor condition from rain and the like, and the Partisans repaired them with logs by laying them alongside one another. The "corduroy" effect was very similar to that employed by the Union troops in the U.S.

Civil War in the area called "The Wilderness."

Escaping an Ambush

We had journeyed down from the mountains north of Fiume (Rijeka) and were about to encounter one of the greatest hazards in our odyssey to date: crossing the main highway and railroad leading north from the city. We waited until everything appeared safe one evening and, under cover of darkness, ran from west to east in pairs, not stopping until we were under cover of the bordering trees. The entire episode required only 15 minutes, but it seemed longer. We continued walking east into the surrounding mountains and finally stopped just as dawn was breaking. As soon as we stopped we heard shots in the distance, which were followed by the appearance of some Partisans with a prisoner between them. His hands were tied behind his back, and he had a dark, sullen look on his face that was accented by a large, black handlebar mustache. They told us they had a skirmish with some Ustashi, deadly Fascist terrorists, and had captured one of them. He was led away after a few minutes, and we never saw him again. Our Partisans also brought in two Italian civilians a short while later. They stated that they were not in the military, and, as Italians, were trying to return to Italy. Although they claimed innocence, they were suspected of possible Fascist collaboration and as such were led away for further interrogation. We never saw them again either.

The rest of the next hour was spent enjoying the remarkable view of the Fiume harbor on this beautiful, sunny morning before we got some well-needed sleep.

My impression of the hilly countryside during those early days was that I was walking through a park. The grass appeared as if freshly mowed (it was actually nibbled close to the ground by grazing goats), and the red clay soil footpath, coupled with the white limestone rocks in the immediate area, painted a picture-book scene in the bright sunlight.

Crossing the Old Border

We were now in a more secure area, and we traveled in the daylight hours on dirt roads rather than on footpaths. We knew that we were inside the old Yugoslav border when we observed the railroad crossing sign that read, "*Kadar svonce svonej* — (When the bell rings —)" or some similar printing. Suddenly a shout of "*Stoj!*" made my heart stand still, and I saw a German soldier with rifle in hand blocking our progress ahead. However, the Partisan guides didn't seem concerned, so we continued forward. It was then I noticed that, although in full German army uniform, his cap displayed a small red star. We later learned that he had deserted the German army after returning wounded from the Russian front. Prior to that he had been torpedoed as a merchant seaman and had also been part of an aircrew that had flown over England.

There were many pastures observed from the roadway as we walked down the mountainside near the village of Gerovo. We noticed a teenage girl carrying a huge bale of hay on an improvised shoulder rack to the valley below. It was soon evident who did most of the manual labor in this area: the women. Maybe it was because of the shortage of men. However, this was not evident by the large number of men sitting around the square as we entered the village.

Coming to the liberated territory in the vicinity of Delnice offered us another opportunity — we saw a movie. I don't remember the details of the film, but I believe it was shown somewhere between Delnice and Skrad and dealt with the Communist cause.

Our stay in the Skrad area was highlighted by meeting our first Allied military contact: First Lieutenant John Goodwin, U.S. Army Office of Strategic Services (OSS). Goodwin served as the military liaison officer between the local Partisans and the Allied base in Bari, Italy. As head of the "Mulberry Mission," he was assisted by some Yugoslavs who, in order to increase their prestige with the local populace (and with Goodwin's concurrence), posed as Americans in the U.S. Army. I remember the one-day stayover because we received some chocolates and long underwear and slept in a soft bed with covers in a private room for the first time in weeks. (Lieutenant Goodwin didn't stay too long in that location. We saw him again in Nadlesk a few weeks later — a German tank rumbled up to his house, and he barely escaped with his radio equipment out of a back window.)

From this point, we were transported over the roadways in a wood-burning truck as the entire region had been liberated from the enemy. A few miles from our final destination, Nadlesk, we stopped in Kozarce and were sprayed with a de-lousing agent, which offered temporary relief.

Finally in Slovenia

As we approached our final destination, we came into a lush valley with the villages spaced approximately a half-mile apart. It was in this area that I heard the familiar speech of my parents who had immigrated to America in 1920. I remembered my mother's words that she repeated again and again: "Johnny, don't forget our Slovene language! You'll never know when you might need it!" Little did I realize how true those words would be.

The third village in the valley, as I recall, was Nadlesk, our home for the next two weeks. It consisted of about two dozen buildings, of which 30 percent were barns, with one main street running through that was intersected by one cross street near the center of the town. One of the buildings was to become our mess hall. The buildings were of smooth-walled, plastered construction (brick and limestone plaster), one or two stories in height, with large tile roofs.

Souvenir memorial dollar bill signed by Partisans and First Lieutenant John Goodwin, OSS.

Meeting with Marija Benčina in Nadlesk.

Windows with window boxes pierced the thick walls.

We stayed in the hayloft of a barn alongside a main house, which was the residence of a woman, Marija Benčina, and her two small children. The two buildings were joined by a common roof and separated by a driveway.

Marija's husband was a member of one of the splinter paramilitary groups fighting against the Partisans — the *Bela Garda* (or "White Guard"). Her reaction toward this unsympathetic attitude of her husband was that she donated her hayloft for Partisan use.

The Germans occupied the land at the head of the valley, which was a few miles distant to the north. This area had recently been liberated by the Partisans due to its strategic value as an embarkation point for wounded and also a receiving point for supplies by air. To maintain control of the valley required substantially higher losses on the Partisans' part than is normal under guerrilla tactics.

A 30-foot wide shallow stream paralleled the road at a distance of perhaps 500 yards the length of the valley. An airstrip paralleled the stream and consisted of 1,500 feet of grass. Oddly enough, an area adjacent to the strip appeared to be more suitable as a landing site (when observed from the air), and consequently, when the Germans flew over they usually bombed this more-likely target. On one or two occasions while we were there, a Fieseler-Storch observation plane came over the area at about 3,000 feet to reconnoiter.

Our meals were usually eaten in the small mess hall and consisted of ersatz coffee and bread for breakfast, a plate of watery soup and bread for lunch, and

Shelter in Marija Benčina's barn, Nadlesk.

some stew and bread for supper. We sat down to supper one evening soon after our arrival, and during the course of the meal the power for the 25-cycle light went off. We were informed that there was no cause for alarm as the Germans who controlled the power house had shut off the electricity. Shortly, someone lit a candle and we continued with our meal while it was explained to us that the Germans occasionally indulged in this discourteous practice until such time as the Partisans, who controlled the dam, shut off the water to the hydro-generators, whereupon the Germans would experience a change of heart and restore power to the village. Sure enough, two evenings later as we were struggling through a meal by candlelight, the electric lights suddenly came on.

The village was not only the staging area for wounded and supplies but also

C-47 (DC-3) loading Partisan wounded at airstrip.

served as a liaison post between Allied personnel and the Partisans. A stuffy, middle-aged British army major and an unscrupulous American army buck sergeant comprised the liaison personnel. It appeared their function was more of a front than practical help. They avoided us, and we returned their courtesy by doing likewise.

There were about ten other American airmen plus six British army escapees in the village. Some of these characters had escaped from northern Italy the previous year when they were still under Italian supervision.

The British escapees did not necessarily relish the idea of returning to their respective units, for they realized that they would then be put back into combat, while the Americans sensed that they would be returned to the USA, provided they made it back to Allied control. One of the Britishers, a gap-toothed fellow, was a colored soldier from South Africa, and he was quite a novelty to the local inhabitants who had never seen a black in their lives. They would often stop him in the street so they could rub their fingers in his hair.

There wasn't much to read, and anytime we could lay our hands on something written in English we would devour every last word. I can still recall one British crime thriller — it was an English conception of an American gangster. One sunny day while I was sitting in front of the house reading, I looked up and saw two of the Britishers struggling to pick up a log that they intended to use for firewood. They obviously were having some difficulty. A blonde girl about 17 years old appeared, noticed their plight, and immediately walked over and picked up the log herself. The two Englishmen looked at her in amazement.

Our hostess's two children were an 11-year-old girl and a boy of about 8. As boys will be, this one had a knack of getting into trouble. His mother had her own system of punishment: She would lock him in the pigpen behind the barn where there was no light. His sole companions until his sentence was served were two large hogs. This occurred about twice per week.

Except for a pail of water in which to wash our faces, we relied on the creek during the warm sunny afternoons for cleaning ourselves. Anytime we were near a stream, we took advantage of the water to drown the lice with which we had become infested. After getting out of the water, we would occupy ourselves while drying by picking off the survivors.

The Partisans could not bring themselves to remove their trousers. They always rolled their pant-legs up as far as possible, removing their shirts, shoes, and socks and strolling out into the water. This was the farthest they ever strayed from their weapons, which were left on the banks. Even when nature called, they took their weapons with them to the outhouse.

Among the commodities that the Partisans lacked were sugar, butter, yeast, and most importantly, salt. The lack of salt led to increased urination on our part. This interrupted our sleeping habits, as each one of us was compelled to get up every two hours or so, scamper down the ladder, and bolt for the outhouse. This was bad enough, but it was far worse if one of us happened to have diarrhea. Witness the case of unfortunate Guy Howard. It was our custom to sleep with all the clothes we owned on our bodies, for there were no blankets available. One night when Guy was in extreme haste, he forgot that the third rung from the bottom of the ladder was missing. Scurrying down as fast as he could, he experienced a temporary lapse of memory, causing him to put his weight where there was no rung. This led to an inevitable chain reaction that ended up with a considerable amount of cursing. The hostess was assured that if she washed his pants she could keep them.

Both of my parents had belonged to choral groups, as did their Slovene friends and relatives, staging concerts, operettas, and other musical activities. I had always taken my mother and father's singing at family and social occasions for granted until I left home and found that other adults outside of my relatives did not engage in this activity as heartily or as often — until one night in Nadlesk. It was early evening and dark as we were seated outside of our sleeping quarters when I heard some sounds a few hundred feet distant. Singing appeared to be coming from one of the corners of the main intersection in the village. Walking closer I made out the silhouette of two Partisans singing *a cappella*. The blending voices struck a respondent chord, and I felt an immediate kinship with the natives, for this was part of my heritage being re-enacted in my very presence as if ordered by my parents.

We were blessed with good weather the entire six weeks that we were in Yugoslavia. I recall one particular sunny day, approximately midmorning, sitting outside of our sleeping quarters in Nadlesk and being aware of an unusual sensation, something in the air. I didn't know what it was at first and stopped whatever I was doing so that I could concentrate. Within a minute I heard a distant rumble, and the ground vibrated ever so slightly. Gradually the rumble grew louder, and I recognized the sound of distant aircraft approaching us from the south. It was at least five to ten minutes later that I caught the first glimpse of something in the air as the sun reflected off the silver bodies flying overhead. It was the 15th Air Force of the USA en route to some enemy target. (Subsequent records indicated that the 15th would have flown over that area on the way to Vienna on August 22.) It required 45 minutes for the entire air armada to pass, as if on review, and I felt very proud of this aerial strength displayed to the civilian population on the ground behind enemy lines.

During the two-week stay in Nadlesk, we were given free rein to wander in the immediate countryside. Tom MacDonald and I walked to an adjacent village and managed to strike up a conversation with one of the pretty young girls. She told us her name was Ivanka and lived in one of the local village homes. We told her that we were always hungry. Somehow, she offered each of us a glass of milk. I don't remember if we declined or not; however, we offered to pay for it with some of our American dollars from the escape kits. We brought back a quart of milk for the other fellows and repeated the trip with the same results a week later.

Bob Marcum was the oldest of our crew, and his birthday was due in a few days. We arranged for a party in his honor by purchasing a leg of veal (unheard of prior to then) from Ivanka and brought it back to our hostess to cook. Our entire crew ate in her house, sharing our good fortune with her family.

Going Home

The second weekend in Nadlesk, the four of us who were Catholics sought out the church in a neighboring village, Stari Trg, to attend services. The church was filled with people, including a few Partisans, despite the fact that some of the local populace had relatives in the *Bela Garda*.

Despite my limited acquaintance with the Slovene language, I was able to follow the sermon, and I was surprised that the priest was denouncing the Communist Partisans from the pulpit (at least that was my interpretation of his talk).

This was my first attendance at a Mass in a month, and I had a deep conviction that something was going to happen. This was justified when our first contact with Allied personnel in Italy came that evening: An American C-47 had landed in the field next to Nadlesk during the moonless night, loaded with supplies and weapons for the resistance movement. It had departed within an hour, its cargo comprised of half Partisan wounded and the other half repatriated Allied personnel.

Another C-47 landed the following Saturday evening. This time it included two passengers: Captain James Goodwin and *Life* magazine reporter/photographer John Phillips. They were to accompany the Partisans on a typical raid into enemy-held territory. Eventually, Goodwin's story was documented in the November 6, 1944, issue of *Life*, and Phillips told his in his book *Story of Yugoslavia*.

I went to church the next morning, August 27, 1944, and that evening two C-47s landed with supplies and weapons. Again, both aircraft departed with a cargo of Partisan wounded and repatriated Allied airmen, including our entire crew. I concluded that it was a miracle and attributed it to my recent church attendance.

Meanwhile, the war storm in the Loz valley had not ceased. German troops were advancing toward Nadlesk, and many a family had to flee into the woods as a result of the enemy bombing villages such as Pudob, Dane, and Nadlesk.

Captain Goodwin and John Phillips had joined with the 15th Partisan Shock Troops, which were part of a general Partisan offensive aimed at destroying German communications throughout Yugoslavia and currently had the task of destroying the railroad bridge at Litija, thus severing the main German rail line between Ljubljana and Zagreb.

The Shock Troops set out on their long march on the evening of September 19th. The next morning, about 800 partisan soldiers positioned themselves above the roadway close to the German strongholds defending the bridge. They awaited for the prearranged Allied air strike to commence. Six Allied aircraft appeared at 4:30 p.m. and bombed the German outposts.

The smoke from the ensuing explosions had not yet cleared when the Partisans, commanded by Captain Jesen, charged the castle where the Germans were positioned. Goodwin, alongside of Jesen, soon found himself in the center of fire and was wounded in the leg. He crawled under a shrub and was given first aid by a female Partisan. The air attack was not successful, but the bridge was destroyed eventually by ground troops. The entire episode closely resembled the mission described in Ernest Hemingway's novel *For Whom the Bell Tolls*.

Returning to the USA in October 1944, we were given a month's leave of absence. A friend of my family was associated with Radio-Free Europe, and I recall being interviewed about our Partisan experiences. I don't remember if the conversation was "live" or taped for subsequent broadcast, or if it was ever broadcast.

After the war I had an opportunity to exchange some of my experiences with an ex-Partisan woman visiting the United States, Naida Kraigher. She visited my parents' home in New York City, and we also met on one or two

Ivanka and John together again in Slovenia.

other occasions.

It was nice to be back in the United States and reflect on all that had happened to us during the war. For us survivors, it was a memorable experience that we wouldn't forget. I was one of the lucky few.

Return

In the summer of 1971, my wife and I had an opportunity to combine my business trip to Europe with our vacation, touring by rented car. This was my first return to Europe since World War II, so we included a visit to Yugoslavia in our itinerary. Fortunately, my father also happened to be vacationing in Ljubljana, Slovenia, in his retirement, and the three of us decided to drive to Nadlesk, which was about 35 miles distant.

We arrived in the early afternoon. I had a slight problem locating the barn in which we slept in 1944, since the adjacent house appeared different (the siding of the house had been resurfaced). Confirmation was verified by the ladder to the barn's hayloft, which had served as our earlier sleeping quarters — the third rung from the bottom was still missing!

I immediately recognized the woman who responded to our knock on the front door. She had aged some in the intervening 27 years but appeared robust and healthy. My father, speaking in Slovene, asked her if she recognized any of us. Glancing at each of us in turn she replied, "*Ne* (No)," whereupon my

Reunion in Slovenia (l. to r.): Ivanka, John, his wife Dorothy, son Richard, daughter Diane, and Ivanka's husband France.

father inquired if she recalled hosting some Allied airmen for the Partisans during the last war. She immediately looked in my direction and, remembering our 1944 conversations, replied, "Your mother comes from Domžale!," a reference to a suburb village of Ljubljana. Although she and her children had survived the war, her husband did not return.

We took advantage of this opportunity to visit the next village and renew my acquaintance with Ivanka, the girl who had arranged for us to obtain the leg of veal in 1944. She had given me a small photograph of herself with the inscription "*Za Spomin* (Remembrance)" on the back. The three of us entered the village and spoke with some of the pedestrians, asking if they knew of the girl and her family. Although a crowd had gathered to listen to our request, no one seemed to know of any such persons. Finally, someone suggested that the "old man" of the village be summoned to shed some light on the subject. A man in his seventies soon appeared, and, after discussion with my father, remembered the persons of whom we were inquiring.

It seems that Ivanka had been part of a group of young teenage Partisans who had lived in one house in that particular village with an old couple acting as chaperons; they appeared to us to be a large family. Approximately one month after our departure, the enemy overran the village and shot and killed every person in that particular house.

Some Later Answers

Edi Šelhaus and his associate, Janez Žerovc, met with me in February 1986 after they had received word that I had been with the Partisans during World War II. They discussed some of the background information and resolved to commence their research on my story.

The next spring they journeyed to Nadlesk to question some of the inhabitants, especially the older ones who would remember the events during the war. They inquired of the villagers if they knew Ivanka Riglai (my interpretation of the scripted spelling) and her family, showing them her picture without success. Perhaps some ex-Partisan women could help them — the girls were closer to one another at that time, and they knew one another quite well.

They located an ex-activist from Nadlesk, Julka, who had known a girl named Ivanka, but she assured them that her surname was different. She mentioned that Ivanka's sister was still alive and lived two villages further on, at Dane, a small village pressed against a gentle slope next to the Cerknica wood at the farthest end of the Nadlesk field. Julka suggested that they inquire about Ivanka there.

Edi and Janez knocked on an old door framed by stone arches. Although the house appeared slightly rebuilt, it gave the impression of an abandoned dwelling. The door opened slightly, and Marija Rigler greeted them.

"Is this your Ivanka?" they inquired, showing her the picture.

"Yes, this is my sister! Where did you get the picture?"

"Can you tell us how she died and where she is buried?" they persisted politely.

"This is my sister," the woman stated once more, "and she lives in Australia, but at the moment she is staying with her daughter in Denmark."

She beckoned them to step inside once her mistrust of strangers disappeared. They related my story and how they had received a copy of Ivanka's picture. Then Marija brought the family album and verified photographically that she was the same Ivanka. She also explained that her true surname was Rigler, not Riglai, and that her present married name was Benko.

Marija promised that she would immediately inform Ivanka about their visit and inquiry. "Anyway," she added, "she intends to spend this summer at Dane."

Edi Šelhaus informed me of the good news and invited me to visit Slovenia once more.

It was Sunday, July 5, 1987, when I visited Nadlesk and Dane again. Ivanka greeted me at her sister's house and related the events that transpired after I had returned to Italy in 1944.

There was an enemy offensive by the Germans and their quisling supporters during late September 1944. They were all over the Loz valley where Nadlesk is located. The enemy knew that the Partisans and their sympathizers were hiding in the villages but could not find them. Ivanka moved high up in the attic where she spent some horrible days. Although she could hear voices inquiring about her, she was never found. A year earlier she had been taken to Ljubljana prison where she had been beaten for her collaboration with the Partisans. They finally released her, and she had returned to Dane where she resumed her work with the Partisans until the end of the war.

After the liberation, she married and had a daughter. After ten years she followed her husband to Holland where he was engaged in business. His professional work led them to places all over the world before they finally settled in Australia.

The mystery regarding the earlier report that she had been killed was also solved. Ivanka had a cousin with the same name who had lived in the village adjacent to Nadlesk. It was the cousin who had been killed in the 1944 enemy offensive.

Chapter 10

A Twist of Fate

In 1944, Lieutenant Bill Crim was a navigator on a B-24 Liberator bomber crew stationed at San Giovanni Aerodrome, just outside of Cerignola, Italy — home of the 455th Bomb Group, 741st Squadron. On the 21st of July, his plane was to lead the Group in a strike against enemy targets in Brux, Czechoslovakia. On that day, they had a radar-equipped plane since they were leading the Group. This meant that in addition to the normal ten-man crew, they had a radar navigator on board. His job was to signal when to drop the bomb load in the event that the target was covered with clouds. In addition to Crim as the navigator, Captain Nixon as the pilot, and Major Lanford, CO of the 741st Squadron, as the copilot, crew member assignments were bombardier, nose turret gunner, top turret gunner, ball turret gunner, tail turret gunner, two waist gunners, and the extra radar navigator.

Early that morning, Crim and his crew mates were roused at about 4:30 a.m.; they then got dressed and went to breakfast. Afterward, they gathered their flight gear and boarded the trucks that took them over to the group headquarters briefing room, which was an old underground cellar with many chairs and a stage where the briefing was presented to all flight crews who were to fly that day from the 455th airfield. (The room also served as a movie theater in the evenings.) Four squadrons were present.

After the briefing, the crews dispersed to special area to pick up specific target kits — maps, velocimeter settings for the bomb load, radio codes, frequencies, and the like — for the navigators, bombardiers, and pilots. Then it was off to the parachute lockers and trucks that were to take them to the "hardstand" (parking place) on the airfield where each crew's assigned plane awaited.

The ground crew who had been assigned to the aircraft had already fueled the planes, loaded the bombs, and started and ran up the engines while the flight crews were asleep or being briefed. They also loaded the oxygen and ammunition and placed the flak suits and helmets on board.

Crim's crew smoked and talked at the edge of the hardstand while the pilots, Nixon and Lanford, conducted their preflight inspection of the plane's exterior. Then they awaited the flare from the tower to designate that the mission was on and they should start engines. They started to taxi toward the takeoff area about 7:00 a.m., with each aircraft proceeding in turn, depending on their formation position after the takeoff. Crim's crew arrived at the end of the runway, ran the magneto checks, and off they went.

They started to climb and simultaneously got into formation. The plane gained altitude going up the Adriatic, and the crew put on their oxygen masks at 13,000 to 14,000 feet. All stations (turrets) reported periodically to the pilot if they observed any peculiar action concerning other planes or their own.

While over the Adriatic, each aircraft in the total formation went through a period of test-firing its guns. Formation position had to be rigidly maintained during this time, or a plane would find itself flying through empty cartridges discharged from the aircraft ahead. It could be a bit testy at that point, because inexperienced gunners on other planes might inadvertently hit another plane.

After they crossed the coastline, the shipping concentrations were reported to Crim as the navigator. He made notes on a continual basis throughout the flight. The crew members reported railroad marshalling yard data along with the location and the time; Crim then recorded all of the information in the logbook. Any other noteworthy data sighted on the ground that could be of use to the intelligence section back at the air base was also recorded.

The bomb raids had intensified from early March. One of the worst air raids had been on March 19, when planes were sent in four groups to bomb factories in Steyr in Austria. But due to dense cloud layers above the target, they had to turn to alternate targets: 234 bombers were re-directed toward Klagenfurt and dropped their cargo upon the Luftwaffe airport, while another 76 bombers attacked industrial targets in Graz. Collectively they had dropped 772 tons of bombs. No less than 12 Liberators had been destroyed above Graz. Two of them had been shot down by enemy fighters, and two had crashed due to a mid-air collision while flying close formation, caused by one of the planes losing directional control after its tail was shot up.

It had been even worse on April 2, when the 455th Group, along with 125 aircraft from other groups, bombed Steyr a second time. They were attacked by at least 76 Messerschmitts and Focke-Wulfs. Above the target they had met fierce and accurate flak. Four bombers were shot down immediately, destroyed by a combination of machine-gun and cannon fire during the first fighter attack, followed soon afterward by the flak massacre. By the time the last bomber had left enemy territory, 20 of the 280 planes had been shot down over the target area, and another 30 barely limped home. In consolation, the gunners from the 455th Group on that day accounted for 27 enemy fighters destroyed, 17 probably destroyed, and 3 damaged.

On June 26th, the 455th Group had experienced another catastrophe when they bombed five oil refineries in Moosbierbaum near Vienna. They had not reached their target when 12 two-engined Me-110s attacked with rockets and heavy cannon fire. Two B-24s were destroyed in the first attack. Just prior to reaching the target, 60 Me-109s and FW-190s attacked and split their serried ranks. Some of the heavily loaded bombers were set aflame and fell trailing black smoke. But the enemy fighters were also paid in blood as they flamed like torches and disappeared from the sky.

The attack did not last long, but it was furious and merciless. One of the German fighters in that violent mess crashed into a Liberator and fell without its wing; the bomber, on the other hand, although set on fire, persisted with the group to the target. Another two continued flying, trailing flames up to the target, where they managed to release their bombs. A minute later they both exploded, one after the other — no parachutes were seen in the vicinity.

Gunners from the entire bomber formation claimed that they had shot down 36 enemy fighters, but of the 36 planes from Crim's group that had started, 10 did not return home.

* * * * *

On July 21st, all of Crim's crew were on the alert for fighters, and Crim reported any flak encountered on the way to the target. However, no fighters were encountered in the air. The crew expected to drop the bomb load at an altitude of approximately 27,500 feet. The pilot alerted the crew via the intercom of their position and to be especially alert. Things were starting to grow tense, but everyone was ready. As they approached the IP, Crim helped the pilots into their flak suits and helmets and put on his own. Everyone aboard did the same (except the turret gunners, who were already set). They reached the IP and turned toward the target. They were then on the bomb run.

Crim stood on the flight deck in front of the top turret between the pilot and the copilot, because there was nothing for him to do now but observe. He was always tense on the bomb run because he was the only crew member who was idle: The pilots were gripping the controls, the gunners were handling the guns, the "mickey" radar navigator was looking through his scope, the bombardier was sighting in on the target — and there he stood in his flak suit and helmet, looking out of the glass enclosure as if they were out for a practice flight. There is nothing so useless on a heavy bomber than a navigator on a bomb run, he thought. It is a helpless feeling, and that day was his thirty-eighth experience with that feeling.

They felt the blast of the cold air as the bomb bay opened. Crim looked back and saw the ground through the open doors. He also saw the bombs in their racks ready to be released. They looked cold and deadly. He was already anxious to get the run over with so that they could turn and head for home, when they could break out the frozen Spam sandwiches and hot coffee, when they could smoke a cigarette at high altitude using the oxygen mask to keep it lit (which was prohibited and dangerous, but they did it anyway and enjoyed it).

* * * * *

Krim — it was a Partisan camp of the military-political staff for the broader Ljubljana area. It consisted of some tents and dwellings constructed of branches amidst the shrubs and fir trees, located in a small ravine 150 yards below and some 750 yards distant from the top of Mount Mokrc.

On Friday, July 21, 1944, the whistling of a blackbird announced the approaching dawn. There were still myriads of stars in the clear sky, although they were beginning to lose their brightness with the nearing dawn. In the woods it was still pitch black. A ridge of hills was faintly illuminated in the distance, but on the other side over the Ig gorge, the peak of the mountain Krim was starting to cast its outline against the dark background.

The blackbird was heard again. It was answered with short, sharp whistles by another bird in some dense shrubbery behind Franc (Frank) Škraba's tent. Very soon it would be dawn.

Instinctively, Frank (Partisan name: "Kovač") wrapped himself in his shabby uniform that offered him little comfort in the morning coldness. Half-awakened by the bird's singing, he pulled his coat over his ears and once more sunk into a pleasant slumber.

He used to lie idle until breakfast whenever he felt safe and didn't have anything special to do in the early morning hours. He especially liked to sleep after a fatiguing day, particularly when he was on his feet until late at night. His duties led him all over the Krim area as far as Ljubljana and onward to Velike Lasče, to Bloke, and even further to Nortranjsko. Frank was a courier for the Partisans, and as his routes required him to travel to all of those places, he had also been involved in many military skirmishes.

This particular day, Frank was assigned an easy task: He was supposed to be the link between Mokrc and Krim, and it would take him at least four or five hours to cover that distance.

He arose slowly and thrust his head out of the tent. He noticed more dew than on previous days. It could still be very fine and warm, he thought to himself. He had always been able to forecast the weather for the day based upon the amount of dew that he observed.

There was plenty of time till breakfast. He descended to the "kitchen" where the cook had already started her everyday duties. He brought some water from the nearby spring and also made a fire with some wood.

Having finished his kitchen chores, Frank proceeded to clean his rather new gun — a Mauser rifle that he was especially proud of and which was valuable. It was a police rifle made in 1943 that he had confiscated while attacking the police station at Ig. It reminded him of the hardship of two years ago when he, a thin 14-year-old boy, was imprisoned at Ig and accused of cooperating with the Partisans. He took good care of the gun in order to fight for better times.

The top of Krim flared up with golden yellow light, and shortly afterward the smaller Mokrc was also bathed in sunlight as was the meadow that was named "Under the Cottage."

Now everybody was up. Frank put his rifle away and glanced at the kitchen more often — the hunger pangs dragged him to the cauldron. He had to hurry in order to stop at other places before arriving at his destination at 11 o'clock, where he would pick up mail and propaganda material.

He was not very keen about the food for breakfast: Once more the meal consisted of hard-boiled barley mush larded with brown flour soup that was hardly salted. On previous trips when he was on his way and deep in the woods, he occasionally stopped at remote homes and received something better and stronger for his stomach. However, he had a feeling that things wouldn't look too promising on this day. By noon he would be well on his way and would have to forage for himself to appease his hunger since he expected to have only the warmed-over barley soup waiting for him in the evening.

He did not feel very well as a consequence of not eating. However, deep down in his pocket there always was a crust of bread — for dessert.

It was nine minutes past the hour and getting warmer. Frank came out of the information officer's tent and, with an ill-tempered gesture, put on his cap. Because of his thick black hair, he did not like to wear his cap; in fact, he liked it most when it was tucked behind his belt.

He wanted to start going on his way, but it seemed a little too early. It was only about two miles by footpath at the edge of a hayfield to the lower post where he would have to wait for some propaganda material that was scheduled to arrive at 11 o'clock.

The Partisans who had been relieved of guard duty were silently stepping around the tents toward the kitchen. Secretary Matija, who was responsible for handing out the mail, noticed that the boy trying to straighten his cap was evidently nervous and ill at ease.

"What is it? Did you get out on the wrong side of the bed?" he asked.

"No, comrade Matija," replied Frank; "I only want to get going so that I can stop at the workshop a little longer. I think that I will have enough of a load by the time I get there!"

"What's the rush? You will be sick of Krim in today's heat. Oh well, go ahead but watch for the quislings. They are becoming more and more active. Be careful downhill around Gola, and watch out! And stick to the woods!"

"Okay," Frank answered curtly and in a better humor as he tried to hide his anxiety about the warnings.

He then picked up his rifle and a bag. For a not-yet 16-year-old boy, a half-hour's distance was only a short walk. But Frank was also cautious, even on such a seemingly safe stroll.

As soon as he left his tent, he immediately disappeared into the thick woods. He stayed close to the tall fir trees and started descending along a hardly discernible path toward some grass patches that sloped rather steeply in the direction of a box-canyon under the northern face of Mokrc. Still lower was the print shop for the political staff.

Moisture from the dew licked at the lower parts of his boots as he approached the shrubbery at the edge of the newly-mown field. He scanned the area to be sure it was safe, since he would much rather descend along the pathway next to the woods for the next hundred yards than crawl among the dense shrubbery.

He reminded himself not to make any noise as he listened to the birds' singing and carefully observed the bushes below him. The birds would be flying restlessly if there were anything strange or unusual occurring. So far, everything seemed quiet and safe.

Frank slid down the grass path, squinting in the brightness of the morning sun as he constantly kept his eyes on the surroundings in front of him. The path curved slowly to the left through some shrubbery before it crossed a slight ridge and descended into the valley.

Farther down and to one side and nestled against the slope was the village Gola. Not a soul was in sight. Frank noticed some white smoke in the distance beyond the slope. He stopped once to listen for strange sounds; he didn't hear the village dogs barking, nor the usual gunfire from the Turjaška road where attacks against the German transports were commonplace.

Frank sat down for a minute to calm down, fix his cap, and tidy up. He had nearly lost his cap while crawling through the shrubbery. It would have been a pity to lose it, especially the five-pointed red star given to him by Partisan Vasilij. Suddenly he heard a hollow, hardly audible rumbling sound coming from far away. Instinctively, he listened to the new sound as it grew louder and louder, spreading over the countryside. No, he thought, that sound is not gunfire; it must be airplanes. He quickly guessed that the sound was coming from Allied aircraft. The Americans will beat the Germans again, he thought as he smiled to himself and continued onward.

When the rumbling of the bombers faded away behind the hills far in the north, Frank returned to the path that led into a gorge that was overgrown with foliage. He walked slowly; it was just past 10:00 a.m., and it was only a few minutes' walk through the hazel trees to the workshop.

Earlier that morning he had thought about the possibility of taking another route — toward Turjak. That way he could have stopped at his mother's, who was in Zapotok on the other side of Kuresček Hill. She worked as a cook there, and surely he could have gotten something more substantial and tasty to eat. Now he was certain that he would hardly have the strength to climb up and down Krim.

He consoled himself by thinking that he might come across some cherries — if only the blackbirds and sparrows had not picked them. He always looked forward to early summer in the higher elevations when the cherries ripened later.

Thinking of cherries, he stepped between the smaller tents in the camp and stopped for a while in front of a bigger one. Yes, Herman the technician was sorting today's mail.

He sat down under the trees on the soft tufts of grass that were nicely warmed by the morning sun. His thoughts returned once more to the ripe, sweet red cherries. He nearly fell asleep when an acquaintance of his addressed him rather loudly and invited him into his cottage. A huge pile of material for the Borovnica area was waiting for him in a shabby rucksack.

"It is so, so heavy today," he remarked as he tried to guess its weight.

Well, it was not too heavy, he thought, although he would have to hurry up to Krim, where he had to make a connection at 1:00 p.m. It was a few minutes past 11:00 when he heaved his rucksack over his shoulders and left the camp with a short "*zdravo* (so long)."

It was still cool and fresh in the woods, but he gradually became warmer as he climbed uphill toward the ridge of the mountain. Soon afterward he stepped once more onto the beaten track cut through the woods, eventually ending in patches of high tufted grass. No one had cut the grass in this area for over two years. The region was remote from the nearest villages, and the enemy very seldom ventured to this wilderness.

Frank stepped briskly as the sun shone upon him with all of its beauty and warmth. He got thirsty and turned at the place where he knew there was a spring alongside the wooded path.

He took a few more steps over the grassy border by the woods and arrived at the spring. There, he relaxed a little and refreshed himself. How cozy it is here, he thought. He glanced upward at a cart-track below the lip of Mokrc to a bare stump located at the point where the track curved from sight. Yes, he thought, that is the spot where I will sit down and rest for a while.

Slightly stooped, he stepped uphill and inhaled deeply once more before he finally reached the top. He veiled his face against the blinding rays of the sun that penetrated with full strength to the sloped fields. Here at the top he liked to look at the surrounding countryside. He stared at Sive Doline below and beyond the slant borders of the woods as they ended somewhere near his native village.

The beauty of the day overwhelmed him. For a while he stood and listened. Not far from the path a jay gave a shriek, and behind him in the trees a titmouse chirped with *tzi-tzi-pee, tzi-tzi-pee*. Blackbirds twittered pleasantly as they flitted among the hazel trees. What a concert! And what a day!

Amidst this rapture an unusual sound coming from the direction of Krim suddenly attracted his attention.

"That must be a plane!" High up, almost above the top of Krim, he noticed a four-engined bomber flying toward him. It must be an Allied aircraft, he thought, since he knew the planes, but they usually flew at higher altitudes and in larger formations. However, this one appeared to be much lower, and it seemed that there was smoke coming from its right engine.

*   *   *   *   *

Meanwhile, the flak was getting thicker around Bill Crim's plane. They could hear it under the bomb bay as the enemy on the ground tracked them. It came closer and closer. *Thwack! Thwack! Thwack!* There is no deadlier sound, Bill thought.

They let the bombs go from the plane — and suddenly they were hit. The inside of the flight deck turned black from the dust shaking loose. For a moment, they couldn't see anything; then as the air cleared, they saw that they had sustained a hit directly behind the number 3 engine. The plane lurched, and it dropped out of formation. The pilot feathered what was left of the engine. The controls were badly damaged, and the craft gradually started to lose altitude. The pilots struggled to keep the plane aloft by throttle control — adjusting engine power to raise or lower a wing. They started to track the formation that was above them by then; the second plane had taken over the lead. At least Crim and his crewmates were out of the flak. Everyone was nervous, ready to bail out on command, but the command didn't come. They assessed all of the damage and were thankful no one was hurt.

Lanford, the copilot, switched on the intercom to tell the crew that they would try to reach the Adriatic so that they could ditch the aircraft. He indicated that the main wing spar might have sustained extensive damage and told them of the control problem. They couldn't maintain absolute directional control, and the aircraft continued to lose altitude gradually.

There was nothing to do but stay alert and wait — and sweat. The crew had never ditched before. Bill Crim's mind raced: With damage, does the plane sink immediately? I never learned to swim very well. Do these "Mae Wests" really work? Will we come in close to the isle of Vis?

The formation had gone ahead. Luckily, no fighters were after the crippled plane.

As they approached the Klagenfurt/Villach area, the pilot informed the crew that they were going to fly close to Klagenfurt and might receive some flak. Their altitude was fairly low at that time, about 18,000 feet. Sure enough, all hell suddenly broke loose. *Thwack! Thwack! Thwack!* They were hit again and the air on the flight deck was black once more. Metal was flying. Again they were lucky that no one was badly hurt, but control of the plane diminished. The pilot announced that they wouldn't ditch and that they should get ready to bail out when they heard the alarm bell. The flight attitude of the aircraft was getting beyond control.

In a short while, the bail-out bell sounded, and the men started leaving the plane. Five of them were scheduled to leave from the flight deck area: first the top turret gunner, then the radar navigator and Crim, followed by the two pilots. Crim turned at the bomb bay door to look back at the pilots. Nixon and Lanford seemed to be arguing about what to take with them. Crim went back and shouted, "Let's go!" They came toward him, and Crim jumped.

The plane was in a shallow dive at about 16,000 feet. Crim had a back chute, which made it easier for him to get around onboard. He mistakenly pulled the rip cord immediately after he jumped and sustained a painful jerk, which felt like someone had tried to tie his legs around his neck. He heard a swishing noise, and it looked as if the parachute canopy was oscillating from the left horizon to the right horizon and back again. Each time: swish, swish. He then realized that the canopy was stationary and that he was swinging like a pendulum from the shroud lines. This soon stopped, and he became aware of complete silence except for a droning noise. He sighted his airplane in a dive, and as he looked, the right wing buckled up (the Brux flak had hit the main spar). The plane immediately went into a spiral dive. Crim watched it fall all the way until it crashed into the ground.

He turned and counted the parachutes. Eight below me, two above me; everyone got out, and all of the chutes opened successfully, he thought. He was impressed with the deathly silence, especially after listening to the engines for several hours. The stillness was awesome. It seemed that he wasn't nearing the ground but was simply suspended in space. The countryside was very green and pretty.

As Bill descended, he soon heard what he thought were rifle shots but eventually realized that no one was shooting at them. It was actually coming from the crashed airplane's guns where the ammunition was burning and exploding. As Bill came closer to the ground he could see a deep canyon, and it seemed that he was going to go into it. He pulled on his chute risers in order to slow down the drift but became concerned that he might collapse the canopy, so he stopped. What he thought was a small bush turned into a big

Airman landing in the top of
a tree.

tree, which he missed, and he landed on a pathway near the very edge of the
canyon. He was stunned as he hit the ground, going over on his back, but the
shock of landing passed quickly. Bill hid his chute in the bushes and went over
the edge of the cliff a short way to distance himself from the path. His escape
kit map confirmed that he was close to Ljubljana, which he had already known
before jumping.

At that morning's briefing, the crew was told that if they were ever in
Yugoslavian territory to seek the Partisans in the high country, so Bill decided
to turn uphill. He avoided making any noise and moved slowly, watching and
listening for any signs of life. In addition to the map, Bill was pleasantly

surprised to find in his escape kit a chocolate bar, $60 in gold-seal American money, a compass, matches in a waterproof container, and a few cigarettes.

* * * * *

Frank had not watched the approaching bomber for more than a minute when he suddenly saw two white balloons emerge from the plane. At first he thought that they were meteorological balloons, as he had seen them somewhere previously. But he soon found that they were used to save the lives of airmen as the bomber started to spin to earth.

The airmen were drifting toward Gola. He was about to rush to them when he realized that they would be drifting much farther from the village, probably toward Zelimlje.

The plane approached like a huge, frightening apparition as it circled over him in Sive Doline. One or two engines continued to drone so that the echoes resounded from the nearby summits. Just as the plane reached one of the mountain slopes, a part of its right wing broke off together with an engine and a propeller and whirled as if were a huge leaf toward the other side of the valley.

The noise of the airplane filled the air in Sive Doline. Suddenly it was quiet after the craft crashed into the densely wooded gorge. Frank was only a few hundred yards distant from the point of impact.

A deathlike silence gripped the countryside. Frank could not comprehend all that had transpired in the last few moments. At first there was an unbearable noise; then everything was quiet as if nature had reverted to complete silence.

Terror-stricken, he glanced at the gorge. What should he do? He remembered the airmen . . . only two of them . . . where were the others? Perhaps they were trapped in the wreckage and needed help, he thought.

He grabbed his rucksack and, taking long strides, raced down the slope to a small plain behind which was a wooded ravine. In no time at all he arrived at the first of the fir trees sheared by the plane. The entire area appeared as if it were devastated by a storm. A short distance away he encountered a part of the undercarriage and wheels. Among the clipped trees he spotted the entire tailplane with a part of the fuselage — it looked as if it had been sliced by some huge shears. A few yards farther away lay the rest of the aircraft.

The right wing was missing, but the left wing was still attached to the fuselage. Smoke emerged lazily from the engines; the hot stinking puff reached Frank. However, there was no evidence of fire. He approached the wreckage.

Everything was calm and quiet; the only sound heard was generated by compressed gasses escaping from the engines. Hydraulic fluids leaked from the severed lines, and the smell of oil and gasoline permeated the air. Frank stopped in front of the broken shell of the fuselage — it seemed like a monster to him. Where were the other airmen?

A ladder-like object protruded from the dark, yawning interior of the fuselage; Frank hesitated for a moment before climbing inside. Everything was scattered around the metal floor, and broken instruments hung from the walls and ceiling. The left waist gun was wedged in the twisted window frame with the barrel bent and stuck halfway into the earth. Ammunition belts were strung from the ceiling, and some cartridges were strewn on the deck. The large yellow rubber raft had broken loose from its compartment during the crash and had filled with air. There was no trace of the airmen anywhere.

Suffocating fumes started to emerge from the front of the plane, and the sound of crackling flames was heard outside of the plane's cabin.

Frank, half-bent, was staggering inside the crashed aircraft when he heard rapid bursts of gunfire nearby as spent bullets started to rain onto the fuselage. He exited as quick as lightning and hid himself in the nearest shelter, for he was convinced that he was being attacked by the Germans or the quislings.

It was only some moments afterward that he noticed that the fire between two of the engines had ignited the scattered ammunition belts and had caused the explosions. After he realized what had happened, he returned to the airplane, picked up some cartridges, and put them into his pocket. He also walked to the other end of the plane to look for crew members, but no traces were found of any of them. At that point the fire started to spread and burn intensely.

He eventually left the dangerous site as he realized that he was still on duty and had to hurry on with his task. It had taken him a long time to inspect everything around the crash site and also inside the plane. His comrades above on the slopes of Krim were surely waiting for him at the preselected time. He had to hurry up as he had a long way ahead of him.

He gritted his teeth as he climbed along the steep wooded slope along the shallow mountain creek and quickly arrived at the edge of the Ig ravine. He stood there for a while and removed his two hand grenades to bury them so that they would not interfere with his descent into the ravine. He did a good job of hiding them as he knew the site very well; he would have no trouble finding them on his return trip.

Taking a few deep breaths of air, he broke into a run as he emerged from the wooded edge and descended along the goat trail into the ravine. He continued to run as it was already noon and he had to cross over Mount Iška and traverse a steep slope on the other side of the river.

He crossed the river bed in three or four long leaps and then climbed another 400 yards uphill. His destination was not much farther, since the rendezvous was selected to be above Gornji Ig at Mačkova field.

Rado and Orač were waiting for him. Still red in the face from his quick pace, he greeted them and started to tell them about the crashed bomber under Mokrc. He showed them the cartridges and a big knife that he had found in the demolished fuselage. While the messengers inspected the "trophies," Frank was tempted once again by the thought of the nice, red cherries in the trees a little lower near an uncultivated field. Orač was interested in the bullets, and Rado was eyeing the fine large knife.

"Boys, let's have some cherries!" said Frank as he turned to them, adding, "Rado, will you climb up there and cut some branches?"

* * * * *

As Bill Crim was making his way uphill, he suddenly heard voices. He worked his way behind a rock for protection, seeking the source of the sound. Then, through the trees, he saw three men. One of them was in a wild cherry tree cutting branches and throwing them to the ground. He then descended, and all three squatted down, eating the cherries. Bill could see a red star on their caps, which he knew was the Partisan symbol. But the immediate question was how to contact them without being shot. Each had rifles that were taller than they were. Bill decided to whistle, and when he did, the three Partisans disappeared down into the tall grass. Bill hesitated and wondered what to do next; he finally decided to keep whistling as he approached. As he did so, the three heads reappeared, and Bill walked into the clearing.

* * * * *

Frank had his rifle pressed against his face and aimed at the source of the whistle. A bullet was in the gun barrel, and the safety was released. Meanwhile, for the sake of precaution, the other two couriers had rushed over the edge of the cliff and down toward the village to place the mail that they were carrying in safe hands, since the whistler could be the enemy and it was much better to disperse. They had reacted the way they thought best without much talking.

Frank remained. He was determined to engage in dangerous action with the enemy, but the worry and anguish weighed heavily upon him.

What if they are Germans?, he thought, remembering that it was only a year ago at this very place that the Germans had ambushed the Partisans. It was terrible; much blood was shed.

His position was not the best one for shooting. Therefore, he removed his cap and put it behind his belt. Like a streak of lightning he rolled over toward the lower field. He proceeded to crawl on his hands and knees in the dense woods and raised his head a little as he prepared to shoot.

A long whistle was heard once more from the area of the trees, followed a few seconds later by another one. At the same time he noticed a tall figure in a khaki uniform step forward somewhat hesitantly.

"*Hande hoch* (Hands up)!" shouted Frank in German, so loudly that it echoed back from the opposite steep slope.

The unknown person raised his arms halfway and stopped. Frank rose slightly and aimed directly at the figure. He wondered if he should shoot. If the stranger was an enemy, he must do it at once — but the man was bare-handed. With his finger on the trigger, Frank hesitated for a second or two.

"American!" the man uttered in a deep voice as he raised his arms above his head. Frank lowered his rifle for a moment. His subconscious was struck by the connection between the stranger and the crashed plane.

"Tito . . . American . . . Partisan!" shouted the man in short intervals as he took a few steps forward. Then Frank stood up and put the rifle on the ground as it was now clear to him that this was probably the airman who had bailed out of the damaged bomber.

The man stood still a few yards in front of Frank, riveting his gaze on the cap stuck behind Frank's belt. His eyes opened widely and his mouth stretched into a broad smile.

"A Partisan?" he addressed the boy as he appeared relieved and came closer to embrace him. Frank shook the bony hand and greeted him heartily. He confirmed that he was a Partisan and tried to make himself understood that they were in a safe place. He also wanted to tell him that he knew about the plane, and he displaying the cartridges he had picked up and taken with him.

At that point Frank whistled and the two boys came back. The meeting was cheerful and friendly. Eventually, they strode toward the cherry tree and resumed eating the cherries. The airman dug into his pocket and brought out a large bar of chocolate, which he broke into three parts.

As Frank knew some Italian words, he started to speak to the airman because he was curious to obtain more information about him.

"*Tu, soldato?* (Are you a soldier?)" he asked him point-blank.

"Yes, soldier . . . American," he confirmed.

"*Oh, tenente — poročnik*," responded Frank in satisfaction, speaking the word "lieutenant" in Italian and Slovene. "*Io sono* Frank, *e tu?* (I am Frank, and you?)" he asked.

"I am Bill. Where are the Germans?" asked the airman, worried about the enemy posts.

"Oh, yes, *Germani-Tedeschi!* Over there," he said, pointing in the direction of Ljubljana.

They talked somehow for a while. When the airman found out that he was in no danger for the time being, he showed with gestures that he was thirsty. He took his plastic bag from his pocket and handed it to the courier Rado.

"Water?!"

Rado understood him and rushed toward the village where there was well water next to a house.

Bill began to trust Frank more and more as he had an inner feeling that he could rely on this bright lad.

"Where — *dove sono io?*" he asked, trying to speak Italian. From his pocket he pulled a folded map that was printed on silken material.

"Krim!" answered Frank as he stretched his arm in front of him and farther up the steep slope. At that point, the airman stood with open mouth, speechless. He finally stammered:

"Crim? I am Crim!" and pointed to himself, full of surprise but firmly, still wondering how on earth the boy, who had never seen him before, knew his name.

Once more, he asked where he was as he spread his map.

"Yes, Krim!" assured Frank, not knowing what the problem was. He bent over the map and pointed to the peak where Krim was located.

The airman still did not understand him and therefore tried to emphasize the point.

"*Io* Bill Crim . . . and you?" he curiously pointed to Frank as he asked his name for the second time.

"Frank!" he answered. "*Monte Krim, hier,*" he said again, using yet another German word to try to make it clear that the mountain over which the airman hand bailed out was called Krim.

It finally dawned on Bill that he had parachuted onto a mountain with the same name as his. Unbelievable, he thought, as he pulled some more articles out of his pocket and shared them with the young Partisans. Meanwhile, Rado had brought plenty of water for all of them. They then took leave of one another.

There was no shortcut across the Iška or along the ravine, so Frank and Bill proceeded uphill. Bill walked with difficulty and gasped for breath on the terribly steep slope. They both rested. Sweat poured down Bill's cheeks as he grabbed for branches to prevent sliding down on the stones underfoot. Wisps of heather did not provide much support, and he was almost angry at Frank for leading him on this wild mountain slope. They eventually reached the top of the ravine and stopped for a moment as Frank retrieved his hidden grenades. They then proceeded downhill toward the Sive Doline.

The sun had already set when they entered the camp called Pod Bajto. Frank introduced the airman to his comrades. They shook hands. At the same time they told him that another airman had been found at Zelimlje and was at the headquarters of the town of Velike Lašče under Gola. As it wasn't far, Crim wanted to meet his friend that very same day.

It was getting dark when they stepped inside the camp. The fire was burning between the tents, and there was a crowd of people talking lively to one another around it. Crim caught sight of a pair of G.I. boots sticking out of a pup tent — the other airman? Crim decided that whoever it was should continue sleeping until morning.

The next day, Crim's meeting with Major Lanford, copilot of their downed plane, was a happy one as they were safe and sound. But although they were happy, they were uncertain of their prospects and were worried about their fellow crewmen. Lanford had observed Captain Nixon for some time until he drifted over the woody ridge and down into the valley. Maybe he wasn't too distant. But where were the others who were the first to bail out west of Krim? They had lost track of them somewhere on the opposite side. (They later found out that the pilot of the Liberator, Nixon, landed near Turjaška Road near a village where the natives found and hid him.)

It was late in the afternoon when they reached the plane wreckage. Bill stared silently at the remnants of the once-mighty bomber for some time, shaking his head. He then looked for the last time at the place where the mission for this plane had ended so badly.

* * * * *

Three days passed. The Partisans took both airmen to Bloke in Novi Vas where they met up with a third crew member, the tail gunner. From there they were driven by automobile to the Partisan airstrip near Nadlesk in Nortranjsko. There they met one other member from their crew. On July 24, they all flew on a special Allied plane to Bari, Italy.

Bill wanted to talk with Frank and bid farewell before his departure from Mokrc, but the boy had already left to perform other duties — rushing through the woods and grassy ridges around Krim carrying important messages. But he didn't forget Bill; he constantly carried the compass and map that Bill had given him and used them frequently.

A month or so later, Frank found Bill's chute hidden near the plane. A life jacket was also close by. All of these items reminded him of the exciting meeting he had had when he first met Bill. He gave all of the items to his comrades back at the camp except for two panels of the silken parachute, which he kept as a present for his mother and sister; it would be useful in those hard times.

The raging flow of the war dragged Frank in its current. He roamed across the Krim woods and meadows under Mokrc many times and survived many hard battles before the cherry trees blossomed again the next year and liberty was in sight.

* * * * *

Airman Bill Crim and ex-Partisan Franc ("Frank") Škraba meeting again after 37 years.

In August 1981, the telephone rang in my flat. It was William Crim — Bill — on the line, and he was calling from Ljubljana.

Later, I called Frank and I told him that I had a surprise for him — Crim had returned! Frank was surprised; there were a few moments of uncertainty and questions followed by a short break on the other end of the line and a crackling sound, then a deep voice was heard:

"Hello, Frank! Crim here!"

Frank greeted him, said a few words awkwardly, and still was not sure that the person on the telephone was the right one. How could they assure each other that they were the persons who had met during the past war?

"Do you remember that meeting on Krim during the war?" he asked Bill.

"Yes — *Hande hoch!*" stated Bill clearly. He also remembered words they used when they talked about his rank and the Germans: *tenente* and *Tedeschi*.

"What about *češnje* — cherries?" Frank questioned further.

"Oh, yes, cherry-tree boy!" the former airman laughed, and so Frank allayed any suspicions he had had about the identity of the visitor.

An hour or so later they met at the Union Hotel in Ljubljana, shook hands, and embraced each other. It was their second meeting, 37 years after the first one between an airman and a messenger boy whose paths had crossed during the war. Destiny had joined them once more.

Bill Crim with a native on Krim.

The meeting was hearty and warm. Even in their wildest dreams they could not have expected to meet again after that quick leave from each other under Gola.

After the war, Bill continued his service in the Air Force and later was employed by the aerospace industry on Air Force and NASA projects. During that period he often recollected the brave and fateful moments of the past. He had forgotten the names and some of the details, but he had not forgotten the boys from the cherry tree. And later he related his exciting war story many times to his children — of how he saved himself from the downed bomber and how he met the Partisans at the cherry tree in the mountains someplace far away.

Some 35 years passed, and Bill had started to plan a visit to Europe, to Yugoslavia. Uncertainty had left many open questions — about places, people, conditions — and the wish to meet his former rescuers had become stronger and stronger. So Crim had traveled to Slovenia with his wife.

When he returned again, Frank, with whom he had been reunited, took all of them toward Krim — to Sive Doline, where Bill's plane had crashed, and farther on to the top of Mokrc, where the fortieth anniversary of the Šercer's brigade foundation was being celebrated. When Crim saw the friendship of old-time soldiers and heard the songs sung at the campfire, he was touched and tearful at the sight of such a display. How great these people are!, he thought and kept staring at the dancing comrades as they embraced one another.

As he approached a group of ex-Partisans, somebody stepped in front of him and studied him. Finally he exclaimed, "William, is that you?"

At first Crim looked at him curiously, and then he recognized him. It was comrade Anton Kovač ("Branco Jereb"), the former commander in whose tent Crim had spent the second night among the Slovene Partisans.

The days of pleasant meetings passed too quickly; Bill had to return to Colorado. But he called again two years later. He was in Germany on business and took advantage of his close proximity, going to Kranj to visit his friend Frank for a short stay.

Bill Crim returned once more in 1987. He stayed in the vicinity of Mokrc at Krim and among the friendly people who had helped him in 1944.

He met with me several times as we talked about the earlier events. He stated that during the second or third day's stay at the Partisan camp, he had written all of them a letter of gratitude for their help. He still wondered if anybody had read his letter and what, if anything, had happened to it.

He also recollected how his airman's uniform had caused some amusing scenes. He had wished to remove the wires from his electrically heated flying clothes. He gestured this to a female Partisan — he did not wish to undress in front of her — and then pointed toward the bush where he was supposed to undress. Meanwhile, the Partisans misunderstood him and his two gestures and thought he meant something else. When Bill returned alone with the wire in his hand, they all laughed heartily. Was that female Partisan Marija Kovač?

Most of all, Bill remembered how the Partisans took care of the airmen and how they shared the scarce food unselfishly among themselves. During their travel to Bloke, the messenger boys offered the Allied airmen a larger portion of their meal, keeping only a handful of cherries for themselves. He stated that he was deeply moved by that incident, so much so that he and Lanford had cut up a piece of bread and an egg and had shared the tiny bits with all the persons in the group. (Bill often told the story in the USA about how the Partisans had given them "the shirt off their backs.")

Only one exciting event had occurred on the way from Krim to Nadlesk in 1944. As they drove from "Bloška Planota" in a horse and buggy, they were suddenly surprised by machine-gun fire. Bullets whistled over their heads and cut some branches from nearby trees. They immediately jumped from the buggy and raced to a house close by for shelter. They drew their Colts and

Thelma and Bill Crim with Edi Šelhaus in Ljubljana.

prepared for action. It turned out to be a false alarm caused by a Partisan who had carelessly triggered the burst while cleaning his gun.

Bill would never forget that horse and buggy. During his first return visit, he immediately recognized himself in the picture that had been taken during their drive toward Nortranjsko. How wonderful it would have been to sit in it again. So Frank — Franc Škraba — invited him on a trip to Bled where they hired the same kind of horse and buggy as Bill had previously ridden many years ago. Bill's wishes were fulfilled.

Chapter 11

A Mother's Remembrance

After my second book, *Zbogom, Liberty Bell,* on rescuing Allied airmen who evaded capture was published in 1988, I received a letter from Anica Kos, the mother of a Partisan:

> I have read your book "Stotinka Sreče" with much interest. It's good that someone has documented the fortunes of some of the lesser-known Allied airmen who needed assistance behind enemy lines. Let them know how the local inhabitants, sympathetic to the Allied cause, risked their lives helping them.
>
> You might be interested in the following: my son, Miljenko, a medical student during the war, was imprisoned in the Gonars concentration camp in Italy. After Italy's unconditional surrender in 1943 he joined the Partisans and was responsible for the medical health of the Dolenjska detachment personnel.
>
> It so happened that one of the Allied airplanes flying over Litija [in central Slovenia] was shot down. Two of the airmen that bailed out of the plane were shot by the Germans. A third was wounded and rescued by my son, who carried him on his shoulders to Partisan territory and safety. After Miljenko administered first aid and the airman was sufficiently recovered, the American was escorted to the Partisan airfield in Bela Krajina. A few days later, on 5 September 1944, my son fell mortally wounded in action at Sv. Kriz [Holy Cross] near Litija [in central Slovenia].
>
> Please call me in Ljubljana. You are welcome to review the pictures and documents that I kept in memory of my son. . . .
>
> Anica Kos

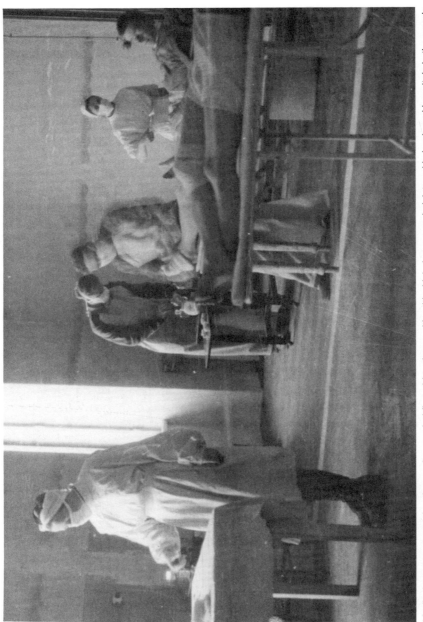

Medical treatment, serving those who needed first aid to those with critical injuries, was administered in bunkered hospitals in the woods under the most trying conditions.

The meeting with the 85-year-old mother was pleasant and informative. In spite of her age she still led an active life and recollected many details from the war. She had many press clippings mentioning her son. She also wrote poetry dedicated to the memory of Miljenko. Her husband had died long before as a result of wounds received during World War I, and she herself had endured two horrible years in the Ravensbruck concentration camp. After the war, a Partisan named "Očka" (a nickname meaning "daddy") had invited her to visit him so that she could learn about her son and the American airman. He related how the inhabitants of Litija and the surrounding hamlets remembered Miljenko as a fine medical worker who also assisted the civilians in that area. They were grateful for everything that he had done for them.

Anica also displayed photographs and letters from America. One stated:

Dallas, Texas 1/21/46

Dear Doctor Miljenko,

I hope and wish that this letter finds you in good health. Best regards to you and your fellow Partisans.

I hope your wonderful homeland and your fine people are in better condition than the last time I saw you. Doctor, I hope you have not forgotten me for I will not forget either you or your comrades — you did your best to help me.

I am one of the Americans you saved and helped during the German occupation. I promised you then to write you if I survived and returned to America. I am fulfilling that promise now. Please, write to me as soon as you get this letter. I'd very much like to help you, send something to you. If it were possible, I would like you to come to America. I would be happy to have you here as my dear guest.

Please, write to me and let me know how you survived the war and how you are feeling now.

Many regards,

Your friend from Texas,
Lt. D. B. Horton

Miljenko's mother answered Lieutenant Horton:

Dear Sir,

It is not Miljenko who received your letter of January 21st but I, his mother. I am sorry to say that he will not be able to read your dear letter. I understand that he, too, remembered you in kindest terms.

Miljenko Kos as a student.

My only son, my golden Miljenko, died for his country and for our freedom on September 5th, 1944, and had been interred in the woods. Then, after my return from Germany where I had been interned for two years, I had him exhumed and transported to our local churchyard.

I cannot describe my suffering as a result of this heavy loss, but there are thousands of mothers who, like me, cry and have no tears left.

Miljenko was in the process of applying a dressing to a girl-

Partisan when collaborators intervened, caught and shot him along with 12 fellow Partisans.

I shall convey your greetings to the group of Partisans who are still living. These have indeed been hard times for our country which you call so beautiful. It suffered immensely as the occupying forces ravaged and destroyed it with their atrocities. The people became poor. Hopefully, the energy of our youth will soon rebuild and restore everything so that our country will rise again and become beautiful once again.

I am glad to hear that you escaped safely and returned to your country. But I shall enjoy it even more if you will come and see me if you ever come to Europe.

I am enclosing Miljenko's photo and ask that you remember him kindly.

In the meantime, please accept my kindest regards to yourself and your wife.

> Most truly yours,
> Anica Kos

After Lieutenant Horton learned that Mrs. Kos's son had died, he sent the following letter:

Dear Mrs. Kos,

It was a long time after I first wrote to you before I received your answer. I had been anxiously awaiting your letter but thought it had been lost.

I was deeply distressed by the news that my friend and benefactor Miljenko is dead. He was such a fine boy and I won't forget him as long as I live. He was the first Partisan to converse with me in English. And how much there was to talk about! He talked about his country and I told him about mine. We agreed that he would visit Texas if he survived. I promised to teach him how to ride a horse like a cowboy. He especially liked talking about food, which was his favorite topic.

I hope you have had enough food to eat by now. Except for the period with the Partisans I have never known what it means to suffer from hunger.

I spent the Christmas holidays with my wife at her parents [*sic*] house. We had a nice family Christmas Eve. As we sat down at the table I thought of you, dear Mrs. Anica. I wished that you were at peace at that moment. It was then that I made up my mind to write to you again.

Lieutenant D. B. Horton and his family.

I still think that we should meet and talk and also meet Miljenko's comrades.

I would like, from the bottom of my heart, to send you some kind of present. Please write to me and let me know your wishes so that I may comply with your request.

Miljenko's picture is in my room. It will be there for good and I will always tell everyone how good your son was.

Many kind regards wishing you stay well. Find enclosed a picture of my family.

Yours,

D. B. Horton

Anica thanked Horton for his letter, letting him know that she did not expect to receive any gifts. Her Miljenko would not have expected any either. But she would be grateful to anyone who would preserve his memory.

When I met Anica the next time, she showed me her poems written in memory of her son. One of them is translated below:

When you were quite a small boy,
You hid yourself in my lap,
And talked to yourself about
The presents you would like to receive.
         You mentioned some goodies,
         You wanted a sled and books,
         Quite silently you whispered into my ear,
         That you also wanted a doll with golden hair.
A doll is not meant for boys,
There are other things for them.
I'll buy you a saber and a gun.
"No, Mother, no, I don't care for them."
         Hard times came upon us,
         And the Slovenes were forced into bondage.
         Fresh gravesites opened up
         To receive your golden sons.

Chapter 12

Good-bye, *Liberty Belle*

After John Hribar had located many of the American airmen rescued in Slovenia during World War II and had assisted in collecting various data and stories of their experiences, I started to receive many more stories concerning rescued airmen, including the following letter:

> Your name was referred to me by Mr. John Hribar of North Port, Florida, USA, who is trying to reunite Yugoslav Partisans with rescued Fifteenth Air Force fliers.
>
> My father was a B-24 pilot who with the crew spent 49 days in the company of Yugoslav Partisans. Recently he and I have been collaborating on a research project about those 49 days. This project might eventually lead to a book.
>
> In trying to collect as much information as possible about their time in Yugoslavia, I am attempting to locate those members of the crew with whom my father has lost touch since the war. I would also, of course, be interested in locating any Partisans who may have aided in their escape. Here is some relevant information on the crew and its time in Yugoslavia.
>
> Plane: B-24 "Liberty Belle" — 304th Wing, 455th Bomb Group, 741st Squadron.
>
> Events: Shot down during the October 7th raid on Vienna. Crew bailed out in the area of Koprivnica. Tail gunner was captured, but the rest of the crew was rescued by Partisans and made their way out of Yugoslavia via Sokolovac, Topolovac, Sv. Ivan Zabno, Dubrava, Cazma, Garesnica, Lonja, Prevsac, Glina, Kladusa, and Obrovac. Arrived in Zadar on November 24, 1944 and, after

several days aboard a British Royal Navy ship, returned to the Fifteenth Air Force.

Members of the crew:

Carver, Harry; Hoosick, New York

Corbo, Nicholas J.; Withersbee, New York (current: Rensselaer, New York)

Cunningham, Elliott L.; Worthington, Minnesota

Dupree, Arnold D.; Laurel, Mississippi

Johnson, Arthur R.; Sterling, Colorado (current: Fair Oaks, California)

Martin, Keith E.; Los Angeles, California (current: La Canada, California)

Maes, Donald; El Monte, California

Merritt, John I.; Daytona Beach, Florida (current: Verona, New Jersey)

Rudolph, G. Carl; Aldan, Pa.

Wheeler, Robert F.; Yucaipa, California.

I would be very interested in learning of the existence of any Partisans still living who assisted in the escape of the Liberty Belle crew. It is possible that sometime in the next two years my father and I will visit Yugoslavia to retrace his steps and to seek out any surviving Partisans who assisted him.

I would also be interested in knowing about any other former American airmen who have been in touch with you and about any of them who may have returned to Yugoslavia.

Thank you very much for any assistance you might be able to give me on this project.

Sincerely,

J. I. Merritt

I was happy to receive that letter. It allowed me to fulfill simultaneously my wish to research the history of rescued Allied airmen as well as to contact the people on the other side of the ocean on the same subject. I offered my assistance and enclosed some photographs of rescued airmen as they were departing from the Partisan landing strip in Bela Krajina.

Jim Merritt works at Princeton University, New Jersey, where he, as did his father, obtained his degree. Jim was satisfied with my answer and was enraptured with my photographs. He showed them to his father, after which they were even more enthusiastic to come to Yugoslavia — much sooner than they had originally planned.

Jim also let me know that he had obtained some books on Yugoslav conditions during World War II. He also started studying the Serbo-Croatian language in order to be able to make use of it while visiting Yugoslavia.

Jim had come in contact with some of the crewmen and would send me some of their statements to assist me in making additional contacts in Yugoslavia. From the American 15th Air Force archives he found statements that the crewmen had given at the debriefing after returning to their base. His father was to meet some of his wartime buddies shortly and would probably learn some new information as they reminisced about their experiences.

In Jim's letter of October 1985 he sent word of their scheduled arrival:

> I am writing to tell you of recent developments in my writing project concerning my father's experiences in Yugoslavia in October and November 1944.
>
> Most important is a decision on my part to come to Yugoslavia this year — in October, which would be 42 years to the month that my father and his crew parachuted into your country. I have made some preliminary arrangements with Pan American Airways on this matter and have also written to the Yugoslav State Tourist Office in New York City for their assistance. Over the next several months I will be putting these plans into final form for the trip to Yugoslavia with my father and members of the crew. We would expect the trip to take place during the approximate period of October 5-14 and to follow a route between Koprivnica and Zadar, with stops along the way.
>
> As discussed in my earlier letters, it would be very interesting — in fact, crucial to my project — to be able to meet with the Partisan veterans who were active in Croatia at the time and with specific individuals who assisted my father and his crew along their route. For example, October 7 is the anniversary of their parachuting into Croatia. Some of the Partisans in the Koprivnica area who assisted in their escape from the Ustashi and the Germans must still be living. Since their Liberator bomber crashed in a fiery explosion on a hillside, there must be people who can remember that, too.
>
> I wonder if any remains of the plane can still be found, and if we could visit the exact location where it crashed?
>
> There presumably are other people still living who assisted them along their route: in the Miklouš-Cazma area, for example, where the British Military Mission had a station; in Garesnica, where they spent one week; and in the Glina-Topusko area, where they spent about ten days before moving to Obrovac and Zadar. [Topusko, of course, was headquarters of both the Croatian Partisans and the British Military Mission of Croatia, headed by Randolph Churchill. Another British officer there was the late Evelyn

Waugh, the well-known novelist, who provides a great deal of information about day-to-day life at the mission in the published diaries.]

As I said, I am hoping that the Yugoslav State Tourist Office in New York City will help me arrange my itinerary. The success of this trip, however, very much depends on our being able to meet with former Partisans and to have as a guide someone who is knowledgeable about the territory and the history of Partisan action in Croatia, and who can speak English. (Within our group there will probably be persons who can speak German and French fairly well, but no one with fluency in Serbo-Croatian.)

I very much appreciate your earlier effort to assist me in my efforts. My question now is, would you be able to accompany us for at least part of our trip and to help in the capacities outlined above? If not, would you know of someone with the appropriate credentials who could? Of course, we would pay for these services and for any expenses incurred on the trip.

In the interest of helping you find anyone who assisted my father's group, I am enclosing an itinerary of their 1944 route and a list of Yugoslavians known to have helped them. It would be most wonderful if any of these persons were still alive and able to meet with us. Perhaps, Mildred Matech, for example, is still living in Yugoslavia and could repeat her role as an interpreter.

It is very important for me to hear from you regarding any success you may have had so far in locating persons who assisted my father's group and to know whether you could accompany us for all or at least part of our visit to Croatia in October.

Looking forward to hearing from you soon — and, I hope, to seeing you in October!

Upon receipt of the letter I immediately requested help to locate individuals and information supporting the rough outline of the story supplied by Merritt.

In *Arena,* one of Yugoslavia's most popular magazines with a large circulation, I published a notice requesting that eyewitnesses to the *Liberty Belle* parachutists' landing send their addresses to the editor and business office. I did the same with the local newspaper in Koprivnica. The editor of *Glas Podravine,* Dragan Desnica, was so enthusiastic with the prospects that he took sponsorship of the effort. A series of articles entitled "Shot Down over Koprivnica" was printed in response to my request.

While Jim Merritt had much success in locating the *Liberty Belle's* crewmen from all parts of America, I impatiently waited to see the effect of my appeal for readers' assistance. It had been my experience after 10 years of researching data for events that had occurred 40 years ago not to expect success.

But this time, to my surprise, I was snowed under with new data as I received almost a hundred letters. They were from Italy, Germany, Austria, Switzerland, and even the USA. Actually, many of the letters were not directly supportive of the event in Koprivnica, but they supplied me with interesting information about the adventures of American airmen in other places.

Meanwhile, Jim sent me two of the most valuable stories — testimonies of his father's two crewmen who were questioned after their return to Allied control.

All aircrews upon returning from that particular mission were asked when they last saw Merritt and *Liberty Belle,* ship #425. This debriefing was standard operating procedure. Their answers on October 7 served as the official account until Merritt's crew returned. The initial conclusion formed by G-2 (Intelligence) was: "One aircraft is missing and was seen at 1347 hours at the target. It left the formation by peeling off to the left. A/C was in no apparent trouble. Personnel casualties were ten crew members missing in action."

Those men who had brought back the original report trooped out of that building not as happy as when they first entered, for another crew was gone. They also wondered if they would be next.

The first account after they returned was written by Arthur R. Johnson. He reported to Intelligence everything that had happened before parachuting. Here is his story.

* * * * *

For us crewmen aboard the *Liberty Belle,* it was a different story after 1347. We had our hands full, and it was our lot to embark on an experience not soon forgotten.

We took off at 1000 hours, and after joining the formation we headed northeast across the Adriatic. By the time Yugoslavia unrolled beneath us, we were up to 15,000 feet. Off to our right were a few bursts of flak, reminders to keep our distance. All went well, and after two hours we started to climb to our preselected altitude. At 1300 hours we were at 21,000 feet, which was our bombing altitude. Far ahead to our left on the horizon we could see a black cloud. We knew that was Vienna and that we would have to fly through that cloud. There were no fighters, just flak, and plenty of it, but we came through with only a few holes.

I was at the left waist gun. With one hand I held my gun; with the other I tossed out "window" or chaff, metallic paper used to confuse the enemy radar detectors when they directed their antiaircraft guns. The bombardier had released the bombs and we were turning away from Vienna. Below me I could see smoke rising from the Winter Haven Oil Works, and I knew that our bombs had hit their mark. We had flown through the worst of the flak, but I was still watchful. This was my third time in the vicinity of Vienna, and I knew about where the flak would begin and end, but this time the barrage hadn't ended. One of the enemy's guns had our range down pat: Four explosions in quick succession jarred me.

That was the moment that I had prayed would never come, but now, after 26 missions, here it was. The gun was knocked out of my hand, and I hit the floor hard. The right gunner did likewise. I didn't realize that my oxygen hose had pulled apart, but it was only for a moment. It was time to get out. Luckily, I kept my headset, and the pilot's voice came over the intercom: "Is everyone okay?" By that time my flak suit was out of the window, my oxygen mask was off of my face, and I was back on my feet. I signaled the tail gunner and hollered at the ball gunner and then pressed the mike button to call the pilot.

"Pilot from left waist — everyone's okay back here. Number 3 engine throwing oil and smoke, number 4 dead, holes in flaps and wings, over." In just a matter of minutes, even seconds, all of this happened — and more.

Later we were able to piece together what had actually occurred. The first burst of flak exploded directly in front of the plane, and the force of the explosion took the top off of the nose turret. The second burst came through and cut the nose wheel and tire in two and made a mess of the bombardier's compartment in general. It cut the interphone lines to the nose of the plane and also the oxygen lines. Fortunately, the bombardier wasn't hurt. The third burst ripped up the underside off the right wing and exploded in the number 4 engine.

That accounted for the holes through the wing and flaps. It caused the pilot to lose control temporarily of the aircraft, but after falling from 18,000 feet to 10,000 feet, the pilot and copilot regained control once more. They used flaps in order to compensate for the loss of airfoil section. The copilot was kept busy keeping the propellers at the correct speed, for the first burst had damaged all of the prop governors. The fourth and last burst entered through the bomb bay and cut through the wing root. It made a hole big enough to crawl through, and the metal is approximately two inches thick at that section. The ball gunner was about a yard away and was not scratched. That was just a portion of the damage to the plane.

Immediately we began to strip and throw out everything that was loose, such as ammunition, guns, and flak suits. That helped, but with only one engine pulling full power it was not enough to overcome the drag caused by the flak damage. We flew for an hour, and then the pilot called on the interphone to bail out. Each one of us checked our parachutes to make sure that they were tight, and then came the word, "Bail out and good luck!"

The nose gunner, bombardier, engineer, and navigator went out through the bomb bay. The right waist gunner was the first out of the camera hatch in the rear, and, to speed him up, we pushed him. Then in quick succession, the tail gunner and the ball gunner left, and I was all alone in the back. The pilot and copilot were up front. I faced the front of the ship and put my head between my knees, and out I went. Of course, that was but a second or two after the ball gunner left. The slipstream caught me, and I went end over end. By the time I had slowed down a bit, I had pulled my rip cord — one long pull. I was jerked straight up and down as the silk billowed open, and I breathed a prayer of thanks for that. The pilot and copilot left just after I did; by the time I was able to get straight, they were also coming down — ten billowy parasols floating earthward. So far we were all okay. The plane did a 360-degree turn to the left with its engines winding up, and then it hit the earth. Seconds after we saw the smoke and flames, the muffled roar reached our ears, and then all was quiet. Deathly quiet.

By the time the plane hit, the first man was on the ground. I came down in the top of a high tree, and after climbing to the lowest limb, I was still about 30 feet from the ground. I could just reach around the rest of the tree trunk, so I slid down and fell the rest of the way. What should I do now? We had been briefed for such an occasion. My chute was out of reach, so I could forget about retrieving it. Down the hill I could see the edge of a small town, so I started walking, but just for a short distance, for I heard someone coming. I had loaded my .45 and placed it on safety as I hid in the bushes with my gun ready for use. A man came along the crest of the hill, watching both ways, and how he spotted me, I don't know, but he did. He didn't take his gun from his shoulder where it was slung, so I guessed that he was a Partisan. He whispered, "*Amerikanski?,*" and after I nodded, he motioned to follow him.

We kept along the crest of the hill at a quick pace and then down towards the west. We met another Partisan accompanying the ball gunner and the navigator. The Partisans tried to talk with us, and by signs we were able to get across that there were ten of us. We took off with one guide, who unslung his gun and motioned for us to form a single-file line and to be quiet. After two hours of fast walking and trotting, we came to a break in the trees; our guide motioned us to follow him low and fast. We crossed a couple of hundred yards to a cornfield and stopped there to rest. Our guide pointed backwards and said, "*Germanski,*" then ahead and said, "*Partisani.*" We knew then that we had been in German territory but were now in a Partisan sector.

After about another hour's walk, we came to a group of houses and were taken to one we judged to be headquarters. There we met the rest of the crew except for the tail gunner. By speaking what little German we knew and using sign language, we made them understand that we didn't want to go on until we found out what had happened to the tail gunner. Orders were given that we didn't understand, and then we were taken to a home and given the first taste of Yugoslavian food — black bread and soup — which was to be our main diet for the next seven weeks.

We were tired and glad to sleep, even if it was on the straw spread over the dirt floor. The next morning at three we were roused by an excited Partisan, and we knew that trouble was brewing. *"Germanski, Germanski,"* was all we could understand. We tightened the laces on our shoes and followed him into the cold, misty, early morning air. It was foggy and pitch dark, so in single file and close to one another we played follow-the-leader. By the time it began to get light, we had covered about six miles over some pretty rough country. We hadn't spoken a word in that time, so when our guide stopped, we began to question him. The Germans were coming to look for us. We still hadn't found out what had happened to our tail gunner.

At about 10:30 we climbed a hill, and just over the crest was a small town. Perhaps I should say, what was left of a town. It was but a skeleton. Ugly walls jutted heavenward, marring the beauty of the landscape, and those few houses that had a roof were hardly fit to live in. The Germans had dive-bombed and then strafed the town. This, we were to find out later, was the picture that was to greet our eyes each time we entered a town. Here we met a Partisan who could speak some English. This old lady had walked some 15 miles since the night before in order to speak with us. From her we learned the story of this one town. We saw the remains of the house her relatives had lived in. They had died in the bombing. Her story could be repeated thousands of times: unnecessary destruction of a helpless and conquered people by the Germans.

That afternoon the ball gunner and I went with a Partisan to another town. He gave us an idea of what we could expect: only a three days' walk, and then a plane would come to pick us up. We were all encouraged. At this town they held a Partisan Congress, and I had the pleasure of speaking a few words. Our interpreter, Mr. Magdich, was very gracious to us and gave us the highlights of the various speeches. I told them that we appreciated their help to all American and Allied airmen and that in Italy the Allied government was doing all it could to secure supplies to be dropped into their sectors.

That night at six o'clock we started our journey, which we hoped would end in just three days. By seven o'clock it was raining, and we were a bit down. By ten we were covered with mud from top to bottom but kept moving, even though it was so dark that we couldn't see our hands in front of our faces. It was still drizzling. We had been going uphill on our hands and knees at times and sliding down the other side, only to continue uphill once again. At about eleven we crossed a railroad track, and at midnight we stopped at a house. We had some hot soup, and though we were wet and cold, we laid down on the floor; before long we were asleep.

At one o'clock the Partisan scout returned, and we started to walk again. It had stopped raining and the moon was shining, so it made the going easier. By four in the morning, Monday, October 9, we met up with a wagon train that was taking some things to the airfield. Although we welcomed the ride, it had started to rain again, making it impossible at times for the horses to move, so we alternately walked and rode until daylight. It was raining steadily, so the wagons stopped for a while. We were tired, but after a rest we continued until almost noon. We came to a small town where we had a chance to dry our clothes, especially our shoes and socks. At two we were off again, thankful that it wasn't raining and that we were partly dry. We also had something in our stomachs: a couple of apples, some bread, and a drink of water.

By nightfall we had crossed into another corps area, so we had a new guide; however, our old one also stayed with us. We stopped to rest the horses and gave them something to eat. All night long we kept moving; part of the time we would ride and then at other times we would leave the wagons in order to circle around a town. This kept up until it was just getting light. We were on the wagons and were told that the airfield was just a few kilometers away. But our gay spirits soon hit rock-bottom, for tracers started coming over the hill. More trouble. The wagons turned around and went back to the small town. The Partisans unloaded the wagons in a shed, and then the empty wagons hurriedly left. Our guide took us to a house and told the lady there to prepare something to eat. In about half an hour he came back, and we left in a hurry. We backtracked a couple of miles and then started to circle around the area where the gunfire was heard and where there was still occasional rifle fire. From our guide we learned the Ustashi had moved in and had taken both the town and the airfield; therefore we continued to the next town.

About noon we were almost at the town when we arrived at a farmhouse. Our guide sent us up into the loft of the barn and told us to lie down. We were glad to, for we were still chilled and our clothes were wet. The sun was warming up the air a bit, so we went to sleep. About two in the afternoon our guide returned, and we had a good dinner of cottage cheese, hot bread, and real country butter; then we were off again. That was the last stop we made until about six.

That night we came to a fair-sized town. There we were entertained like kings and were told it was about 20 kilometers to the next town, where the airfield was located. From 9:00 p.m. to about 3:00 a.m., we rode in a wagon while it rained and drizzled. We were rewarded, though, for when we got to this town we found it was headquarters and they were prepared for us. We had steaks, and did they ever taste good. We were glad to stretch out on the straw spread over the floor and get some sleep. We were bedded down in five rooms of the barracks and were thus undisturbed for a few hours.

We awakened about 10:00 a.m. and wandered outside to see what kind of town we were in. Wednesday morning the sun was shining brightly, and it felt

One of the crew members giving a speech to Partisans.

good to let it warm our bones.

At about noon an interpreter came from the airfield, and we started what we hoped would be our last mile — it was actually about five. There we were met by an English captain who saw to it that we had a place to sleep; he took our names and some additional information. He left us with the promise that this information would be radioed to Italy immediately. We felt better.

We stayed at this field for the rest of the week, hoping that the rain would stop and permit rescue aircraft to land, but no luck. Men from two other crews joined us on Sunday the 15th, and on Wednesday we headed south again in hopes of making the coast. From Sunday night till Wednesday, when we arrived at this airfield, we had traveled approximately 75 miles measured in a straight line. By road we had covered about 150 miles. We didn't know at the time what we were to encounter; if we had, we probably would have given up long before we started. Ahead of us were two 36-mile forced marches, part of the time under fire. There were 26 of us who made those miles, and each mile saw 26 men wishing it was the last. Rain, mud, cold, little food, no sleep; it all added up to make each step harder to take.

The first march carried us over the main rail lines between Belgrade and Zagreb (after the Partisans had blown up the train and track) and over two rivers. It started at six in the evening, and at noon the next day we stopped across the river. Most of the time we were in danger of being attacked. The second march started after one night's sleep, and it took us across another river and two railroads after we had traveled one day and one night. I don't know what happened the last eight hours of that march; the flu had caught up with me and was doing its best to put me out of action. We were still 200 miles from the coast after walking most of the previous 250 miles. Fortunately, the next 200 miles we were to be transported by truck. On the 22nd of November, we reached the coast and were taken aboard a British flak cruiser. On the 24th we crossed the Adriatic by PT boat, and on the 26th we were back in our squadron ready to come home. Behind us were seven weeks of experiences that were fast becoming only dreams.

* * * * *

Navigator Carl Rudolph described the end of *Liberty Belle* thus:

> All this time we headed south, west of Lake Balaton and then over the border to the nearest Partisan area in Yugoslavia. The last checkpoint I remember was the junction of two rivers [the Mura and the Drava], which marked the boundary between Yugoslavia and Hungary. Ten minutes later we passed a few miles west of Koprivnica and bailed out in the hills. Martin was the first out, then Corbo, myself, Maes, and last, Merritt.
>
> My chute snapped open on the second tug, and then I was hanging in a straight line with the rest as the *Liberty Belle* sped away. Two more chutes popped after me. Then the plane slowly banked to the left and appeared as though it might be coming around after us, but it continued to turn and finally plunged into the side of a mountain in a ball of flame. We had ringside seats for that sight — and so ended the combat career of the *Liberty Belle*.

Rudolph's account was similar to Arthur Johnson's up to the point when the crewmen were separated in Dubrava. John Merritt and Carl Rudolph had the good fortune of staying with a local doctor. On or about the 24th of October, he and his companions joined a small army of Partisans and moved out of Miklous later that afternoon. Rudolph recalls:

> As usual, the weather turned bad, and it rained the whole night. The night was so dark I could not see my hand in front of my face. We walked along with hands on each other's shoulders in order to keep in contact. Early on the morning of the 25th we reached Popovac and slept in a house on the floor. The next morning I awakened with chickens walking all over me, the ones that lay

eggs. We didn't have any eggs for breakfast, however, but ate some pig lard mixed in corn meal — not very appetizing.

Early on the morning of the 26th they were on the move again and reached Srp Selišče in the afternoon. The following day the Partisans killed a cow, and they enjoyed the steaks so much that even the sound of machine-gun fire had little effect on them.

Rudolph mentioned Garesnica, the town they reached by night:

We remained there for approximately a week. Our stay here was uneventful except for a chicken dinner I had one afternoon at a local farmhouse. Another day we heard some shots, but it was only a few soldiers chasing an escaped pig which was about to be slaughtered.

He also wrote about Merritt's hand that had become infected and for which he was sent to a hospital near Topusko, about five miles west of Glena. Merritt stayed there about a week and came back in much better humor and with his hand in good shape.

Arthur Johnson concluded his account with these lines:

Today I look back on these experiences and know that through no power within myself I am at home. God in a marvelous way kept His guiding and protecting hand over us.

* * * * *

After Janez Žerovc looked through all of the information received recently from various parts of Yugoslavia and had selected the most important items for our *"Liberty Belle"* chapter, we paid a visit to the individuals who had supplied us with the information so that we could verify and check their statements. It was only after this effort was satisfactorily completed that we decided to invite the Merritts to come to Yugoslavia to visit the plane crash site.

It had taken us more than a year to get everything ready before we finally shook hands with them at the Hotel Intercontinental in Zagreb on September 2, 1986. Yugoslavia at last! Destination: Koprivnica.

While Jim drove their rented car, his father studied the villages, hamlets, scattered homesteads, and people with much interest. He was impressed by the sight of endless fields of corn ripening under a flawless September sky. In 1944, the countryside had reminded John Merritt of Piedmont, Virginia, and now his son remarked likewise. John did not remember Vrhovec, Dugo Selo, or Križevci, because 42 years ago he walked past them at a safe distance,

John and Jim Merritt on the outskirts of town.

avoiding the strong enemy outposts.

The editor of the local newspaper, Dragan Desnica, informed the townspeople of our arrival. Among those present were Partisans, including Branko Vitanovič, who was the commander of this area during the war and whose responsibility it was to take care of the Allied airmen. Our visit was not an official one; it was just a relaxed meeting with the Allies who shared the same destiny with the Partisans so many years ago. Journalists and photographers of several newspaper editorial offices and a TV news crew were present to record an exceptional meeting in a cordial atmosphere.

Jim Merritt described their meeting with all those people in his article published in the October 29, 1986, issue of the *Princeton Alumni Weekly:*

> Edi Šelhaus' articles have made my father a celebrity, and his appearance was a media event. Newspaper reporters and photographers and a TV news crew followed us into a meeting hall where we assembled around a large table with officials of the local veterans organization and the first of several former Partisans who assisted in the crew's rescue. After exchanging war stories, we toasted the

occasion with a round of "rakija," an indigenous plum brandy with the clarity and potency of pure grain alcohol. "I am very grateful for the assistance we got here in October 1944," my father told them. "Without it, we might not be here today."

Branko Vitanovič, who was commander of the Kalnik area, said:

> There were many Allied soldiers crossing our area. Some of them were escapees from German captivity; others were airmen. A lot of them came from nearby Slovenia by courier connection. They were Englishmen, Americans, Frenchmen, and Russians. Some of them were also wounded. I remember a wounded American airman who was not from your bomber. He died and was buried in Poganjac. We helped all of them with clothes, food, and medical treatment, but our prime purpose was to escort them safely to the next area. I remember the crewmen who bailed out over Koprivnica quite well. "Tito — Partisans" were the most frequent words we uttered, as we did not know any English. One of them gave me his Colt in exchange for an Italian Beretta.
>
> Tell the airmen in America that the Partisans of Kalnik area send them greetings hoping to see them here in Yugoslavia. We will receive them with hospitality as we had received them long ago, but this time, for our pleasure, it will be under different circumstances.

Additional townspeople and cars from other areas started to accompany us and the reporters, anxiously waiting for the meeting between the rescuers and the *Liberty Belle* crewman. At Milan Suka's house, four generations of Suka's female relatives — his aged, black-shawled mother-in-law, his wife, his daughter, and his granddaughter — were waiting for us. Milan Suka had been among the first Partisans who ran towards the parachutists to help them. Milan and John did not recognize each other at first. However, from the ensuing conversation during which the 1944 event was described in detail, it was obvious that they were talking about the same things. Their concluding greetings, handshakes, laughter, and pleasure were followed by the surprise of the evening: The hostess served the guests real *podravski struklji* (similar to hot strudel). Anyone who had had the memorable *struklji* in Yugoslavia in times when there was scarcely any food for survival never forgot it.

Next, the entourage visited Žarko Gudek in Koledinac where festivities were being prepared in honor of the Merritts' arrival. Žarko and John looked at each other for a moment, and then they flung themselves into a warm embrace. Žarko exclaimed: "How are you, my comrade? I'm so happy to see

First meeting between John Merritt and ex-Partisan Žarko Gudek.

you here amongst us, so glad you managed to visit us so that we could reminisce about those hard times, but at the same time good times, when you in America and we in Yugoslavia fought for the same cause."

Everybody listened attentively while Žarko recalled the events of October 7, 1944:

> I and my comrades came from Vrhovec and rested on the peak of the mountain above Subotica. As we curiously watched the waves of American bombers returning from Austria, I noticed a plane that was flying well behind the others and much lower than the rest. Anticipating that the plane would probably crash on or near the border between Ustashi and Partisan territories, I stationed my men strategically for a rescue attempt.

> Moments later some parachutes ballooned in the air, so I turned to my comrade, Feliks Kučan, who I knew was the fastest. I ordered him to run quickly to our headquarters to get some extra help lest the parachutists fall into enemy hands. Feliks did not have to run all the way, for he met a group of his comrades halfway there. When they returned, I organized them and asked the natives to cooperate with us. There was hardly any time left as we heard that the enemy was close. In record time all parachutists were collected

Partisan Žarko Gudek at the time of the rescue.

except for the tenth one, for whom we were a little too late. It was the tail gunner, Carver, who fell into the Ustashi zone and was captured.

Then Žarko left the guests alone for awhile, but soon he returned with a gold lapel pin that was a facsimile of Yugoslavian leader Marshal Tito's signature. He pinned it onto John's jacket, saying: "Tito! Tito was a word of recognition, so let this lapel pin be yours in memory of the statesman who was also respected and appreciated in the USA."

In the *Princeton Alumni Weekly,* Jim Merritt wrote:

> The late communist leader is Yugoslavia's George Washington and Abraham Lincoln wrapped into one, and . . . in almost all of the houses we visit[ed], an official portrait of him hangs on the wall. My father is a staunch Republican — In October 1944, when Partisans shouted at the Americans "Roosevelt! Roosevelt!" he would shout back "Dewey! Dewey!" — and no lover of the communist system. Nonetheless, he found much to admire in the courage of the Yugoslavs, who alone among the East European communities declared their independence from Moscow following the war.
>
> "You are the only country I know that told both Hitler and Stalin

to go to hell," he told them. "What other country can say that?"

At parting, Žarko's strong arms embraced John. John then hurried to his car and unpinned from his jacket a badge representing the Liberator, the plane he had flown in, and pinned it to Žarko's shirt.

The news of the Merritts' arrival at Koprivnica spread throughout the area, reaching many who had been in contact with Americans during the war. There were so many invitations to people's homes that it was impossible to visit all of them. As several American Liberators had crashed in this area, it did not matter which specific airmen were visiting; the only thing that mattered to them was the fact that they were Americans. But on the other hand, Merritt could not refuse visiting those persons with whom he had first made contact during the war. One of them was Milka Dražina from Podravska Subotica who, before their arrival, described her initial contact with Merritt to Janez and me:

> It was beautiful, sunny weather, and we were in the middle of the grape harvest. The grapes were plentiful. Among the vines people were laughing and singing merrily, as cheerful as everybody usually was during the vintage season. We were already used to the airplanes flying above us. We liked watching them because they represented hope for us, for our people, and the end of the war seemed to be so near. After another hour we heard the planes once more, but this time something unusual happened: One of the airplanes was flying low, and soon afterwards we heard it crash in the nearby forest. At the same time we caught sight of some parachutists. One of them [possibly bombardier Keith Martin] landed right in front of Košuta's wine cellar, which he entered after he got rid of his chute. In the cellar was a large vessel full of fermenting grape juice; he ladled some of the new wine with a small pail and drank some of it. He was a tall and handsome man. The other [radioman Robert Wheeler], who landed not far from us, had cut his hand. His wound was treated and bandaged by a native woman who was picking grapes. They were young boys, a little excited but glad that everything turned out well. We kept smiling at one another and repeating the words that the Americans used when they spoke to us.

"If they really come to Yugoslavia," she said, "you ought to bring them here. We would be most happy to see them again. Give them our best regards," she had added at our parting.

Now, Milka anxiously waited for them on the threshold of her home, hoping to recognize the American whom she had met so long ago. When the Merritts finally arrived, she stretched her arms towards John. They faced each other for a moment and then embraced each other heartily.

Then Milka brought forth a piece of iron. It was the object her father had found in the woods where the plane had crashed. We all looked at the souvenir that Milka had kept in her house for 40 years. When John confirmed that the piece of iron really belonged to the crashed plane, she felt happy. Like the others, she asked Jim and John to tell the rest of the crew that they were all invited to come and visit her.

Our next stop was Bjelovar where we were expected by a physician, Dr. Lidija Ježek-Chytil. Carl Rudolph and John Merritt had found safe shelter during the war in the house of her father, who had died several years after the war. The elder Dr. Chytil spoke excellent English and was a Partisan sympathizer. He had been pleased to host the two airmen who had brought additional news from the outside world. That particular evening had included the luxuries of a hot bath and the only decent meal during John's 49 days in Yugoslavia.

Lidija took the day off for this occasion. Although she had been only ten years old, she remembered and related many details from that first meeting. John Merritt praised the good doctor and was grateful for his help in risking his own life as well as the lives of his family.

Lidija showed them a big map on which her father, after listening secretly to the radio news, used to draw the Allied fronts in the east and the west. She surprised everyone when she placed a tiny pocket compass in a brass casing in front of John Merritt. It was the gift that John had given her father more than 40 years ago. At parting, Lidija was invited to come and visit the Merritts if she ever came to the USA.

Our next destination was Čazma, center of Croatian resistance, where the *Liberty Belle* crewmen stayed for several days. It was also the location of an airfield originally used by Partisan airplanes prior to use by Allied aircraft. But at the particular time in 1944 the planes could not risk landing because the ground was too soft due to several days of continuous rainfall. We found a cottage where the British military mission was headquartered. John Merritt and his comrades had reported there every day, eagerly trying to find information on their departure time.

We visited Glina, a liberated town near Sisak, where the Americans had also stayed for a few days, and where John Merritt had talked to Randolph Churchill (the son of the late prime minister Winston Churchill) who commanded a joint Allied mission. John Merritt also recalled seeing a film starring Robert Young at Glina.

Photographers, reporters, journalists, and TV cameramen followed us continuously. They were rewarded when we came to Vrhovec — where the

L. to r.: Janez Žerovc, Jim and John Merritt, and Branko Herak at the crash site.

crewmen first realized that they were safe after parachuting and where they spent the first night. People in their vineyards and fields stopped working in order to greet John Merritt. Both old and young assembled around us. At the sight of ten-year-old boys, John said, "Unbelievable and yet true — we Americans could not believe that even such boys could fight, carry heavy arms, and continue battle after battle."

One of the persons present motioned to a small house and told us an old cow shed had previously stood there. The Americans were supposed to have hidden there on their first night. John stepped aside from the group and viewed the fenced yard as he tried to remember the place, but he replied that he really could not remember if that was the place where they had stayed overnight. He had some recall after Tina Pariž told him some details.

There were both old and new stories, including some that were obviously invented. Jim wrote everything down in his notebook.

The villagers were loafing about despite the fact that their workday had been interrupted. Some offered to accompany us to the site of the crashed plane. John and Jim became almost impatient — they wanted to get to the crash site as soon as possible. No wonder, for that was the prime purpose of their journey.

We all agreed on the villagers' proposal to take Drago Handžek and Branko Herak from Vrhovec with us. Our convoy of cars drove along a steep logging

John Merritt's farewell to Yugoslavia in 1986.

road that led us deep within a lovely beech and oak forest. We parked our cars at the end of the road and followed Branko and Drago on foot. We hiked along the ridge through an undergrowth of grass and ferns and, after a few minutes, paused at the top of a ravine.

John and Jim were silent, and I perceived that John was excited. He could not hide it even as he tried to pretend to keep cool. We stopped at a place where the forest thinned. At that point our two guides exclaimed in unison: "We are there. This is the place where the plane crashed!" We stood still in silence and examined the crash site for any traces of the wreckage that would confirm that statement. Then Branko told us that the last large part of the bomber, a wheel, was removed some years ago.

Janez interpreted what had just been said. John listened attentively without moving, lost in thought. To the repeated question, if there were any doubts, he finally answered, "Yes, I'm sure we are at the right place." Then he waved toward the trees that were perhaps half the height of the others that reached upwards of 60 feet in the surrounding forest. Soon afterward, everyone was among the bushes, shrubbery, and trees looking for the tiniest remains of the plane. The only one who did not search for anything was John. He stood at one of the trees and stared past us for a long time. No one, not even his son, wanted to disturb him. As I watched him I felt I knew what he was thinking: More than 40 years ago he had been lucky in that he did not die in the plane and that he had landed among the Partisans. While everyone was feverishly searching, John remained motionless and buried in deep thought. I do not know if he believed in God, but I think he was praying, giving thanks for being endowed with good luck. His son Jim had been only six months old when his father had first met the Partisans; now he was here to write his father's story.

My thoughts turned back to the times when I was a Partisan in the Škofja Loka woods, in Primorsko, Bela Krajina, amidst the merciless war. "Edi," I said to myself, "you too were lucky; otherwise you would not be here today."

John snapped out of his thoughts as I approached and became the old John that I gotten to know during our trip. There was, however, one change he could not hide — his eyes were moist. Then he smiled again and, slapping me on the back, said, "Edi, it's a nice day today, isn't it?"

Chapter 13

The Piškera Field Hospital

One of the numerous letters that I received from the USA describes a mission that occurred on October 17, 1944:

> During the re-union of the Army Air Forces 464th Bombardment Group I learned that you wanted information about any American aircrew members that were helped by the Partisans.
>
> My crew and I were on a mission to Vienna on October 17, 1944. The flak was heavy over the target and we sustained much damage to our aircraft. We managed to reach the northern part of Yugoslavia at which time, with the fuel running low, I decided to have the crew abandon the aircraft rather than attempt to cross the Adriatic.
>
> All of my crew, one observer and I bailed out successfully. Two of my crew were captured (Frank Pierce and Kenneth Collum) and they spent the rest of the war as prisoners of war in Germany.
>
> On landing I broke my leg. Within 10 minutes or so I saw a little girl appear and then 20-25 men and women. Realizing that I was an American pilot they were very friendly and ultimately took me to a village in the hills. After a short time several of my crew were also brought in. Within the day all of my crew, except the two that were captured, were together again.
>
> The Partisans were most friendly and gave us the best of their meager food supply. During the next several days the Partisans helped us to reach the coast, tracking at night at times, and hiding us in attics and the holds of fishing boats.
>
> At one point because of my broken leg I rode a donkey at night

Charles J. Salivar in the USA.

over one mountain and was carried on the back of another Partisan over another mountain. To this day I don't know how he managed to carry me up and down that mountain during our march to the sea.

A stretcher was constructed for me, and I shall never forget that a young Partisan woman insisted on carrying the stretcher ⋯ ⋯ ⋯ men.

We finally reached a church near the sea that was being used as a hospital for the Partisans, and we remained there 1-2 days at which point a British gunboat arrived and took us to the island of Vis. I believe I spent one or two nights in a British field hospital on the island and then was flown to Italy in an Army Air Force C-47 with my crew and others that had been helped by the Partisans. I was taken to a hospital in Bari, but my crew returned to our squadron.

Because of my broken leg it was necessary to return me to the U.S., but the remainder of my crew continued to fly against the Germans.

I have always had a fond memory of the wonderful people that helped us. My wife and I visited Yugoslavia in April 1984. We drove from Dubrovnik to Split, Zadar, Plitvice and Zagreb, hoping that perhaps I could recognize some places that we had been. However, it was not possible, but we thoroughly enjoyed our visit to your wonderful country.

My crew consisted of the following men:

> 2nd Lt. Charles J. Salivar — pilot and commander
> 2nd Lt. Thomas Keating Jr. — copilot
> 2nd Lt. Harvey L'Hommedieu — bombardier
> F/O Russell J. Aungst — navigator
> Cpl. Victor M. Nye — crew chief and top turret gunner
> Cpl. Donald E. Harder — radio operator and waist gunner
> Cpl. Kenneth D. Collum — ball turret gunner
> Cpl. Frank R. Pierce — nose gunner
> Cpl. Harvey D. Wilkinson — waist gunner
> Cpl. James E. Becker — tail gunner

I would be pleased if in your researches you discover the location of that little church. I know that we were a considerable distance inland and had to cross several mountain areas and lakes or perhaps arms of the sea. During the time we were there we did not have a map so we could not locate ourselves.

I wish you success in compiling and publishing your book. I would very much like to purchase a copy when it is published.

If I can be of any further help, please do not hesitate to let me know.

Sincerely,
Charles J. Salivar

I wondered who I should write to, as the only real reference was the church above the Adriatic coast. There were several similar churches, but the statement that it had served as a hospital might be something special. I referred to my acquaintances in Dalmatia who had helped me before with similar cases, but this time I had no success. Many of the Partisan veteran organizations in the coastal region provided me with a great deal of information, but nothing resembled the set of conditions described by Salivar.

I also wrote to the editor of the illustrated magazine *Arena* in Zagreb, a weekly with a very large circulation much read in Dalmatia. The readers of this magazine had helped me reach a successful conclusion once before.

I asked editor Steve Mandus to help me, and he agreed. At the beginning of 1987, the letter of the American pilot was printed in *Arena*. In the next month I received several letters regarding the rescue of American airmen, but none contained any clues that could be used to confirm Salivar's description.

We had just about given up hope of succeeding when a letter was received in Zagreb with the following information:

> My name is Ljuba Erak Mijat. During the period mentioned in *Arena* I was a nurse in a Partisan field hospital, that was located in the central part of the Adriatic — or better still, in the Kornati Bay. The place is called Piškera. There is an old church, but during the war wounded Partisans were being received there as well as the elderly and children that needed help. I remember quite well when a wounded American pilot was brought to us. He suffered in pain from the bone in his leg that was broken into small pieces. At that time I was alone — the doctor was not there — so I eased his pain by giving him some morphine. After a short time a British gunboat arrived and took him to the island of Vis. I can also tell you that the wounded flier was very grateful and gave me his address. Unfortunately, I lost it.
>
> I am now retired and live in Zagreb. I am surprised that the pilot remembered the hospital and I am very happy that he is still alive. Please write to him and let me know whether or not he is in fact that pilot who was with us in Piškera.
>
> Best regards,
> Ljuba Erak Mijat

I sent Ljuba's letter overseas, and soon afterward I received a response:

> I very much appreciated receiving your letter of March 20 and the enclosed picture of the church on the island of Kornati. This is indeed the church-hospital that I was in in October 1944.

Ljuba Erak Mijat when she was a nurse who helped an American airman, and 42 years later when she learned that her patient was still alive.

After all these years it is surprising that Ljuba Erak Mijat remembered that she treated an American pilot. All of the Partisans were most helpful to me and members of my crew as they guided us through the mountains to the coast and to the church. A

British gunboat did transfer us to the island of Vis, after which a plane took us back to Italy.

I've often thought about my experiences with the Partisans, and how many American air crew members they saved from capture by the Nazis, at risk to themselves.

I would appreciate it if you would let Ljuba know that I am pleased to hear that she is still alive and I hope, well. My wife and I were in Yugoslavia in April 1984 and we travelled near the coast of Zadar, but I could not be sure where the church was. We also visited Zagreb at that time, and it is too bad that the information about Ljuba Erak Mijat was not available then so that we could meet her. Please give her my best wishes and thanks for remembering an American pilot now 64 years old.

My thanks to you also for your interest in my story and for your interest in the activities of the Partisans and the Americans that they helped.

Sincerely,
Charles J. Salivar

I visited Ljuba where she lives in the suburbs of Zagreb. She was pleasantly surprised at the message with good wishes from America. She then told me more details.

When Yugoslavia was attacked and occupied in 1941, she was working at a Šibenik hospital that had an intensive care ward where the Partisan wounded were treated. Her husband, Maksim, was also employed there. They were both active in the National Liberation Front from the beginning of the war. When the occupying forces learned of her political sympathies, she fled and became a nurse in the 3rd Dalmatian brigade. She was a participant in the famous Battle for the Wounded on the river Neretva,[3] in which she was both a nurse and a fighter. After she finished a special course on the island of Vis, she came to the islands of Kornati, where she did humanitarian work in the abandoned church in Piškera.

She recollected that ten or even more wounded and battle-fatigued personnel were brought to the hospital daily. Piškera was an in-between station between Vis and the coast. Several thousands of the wounded in need went through the hospital, from which they were taken to Vis. She remembers Mr. Salivar had given her some money. She did not want to accept it, but he insisted and she took it. She used the money to buy a needle for her sewing machine.

Charles Salivar received the pictures of Ljuba a month or so later and sent me some photographs of his own. He also sent his regards and added that if he and his wife returned to Yugoslavia, they would try to see me and Ljuba. His last letter was dated August 10, 1987.

This story of an American from Missouri and a nurse at Piškera, now living in Zagreb, took place in one of the most beautiful parts of our country. The two participants of these heroic events will treasure the memories of those moments of exceptional comradeship, loyalty, and help in need during the most trying times in our history.

Chapter 14

Ribnica: Three Stories

Toward the end of October 1979, a car with American registration stopped in the middle of the square in the town of Ribnica in Dolenjska, an area in the southern part of Slovenia. Four passengers emerged, curiously viewing their surroundings. One of them, an elderly sun-tanned man clad in sportswear, was clutching some printed papers, which he showed to the first person that he thought might help him. The information in the papers had been translated into the Serbo-Croatian language by an acquaintance of his in the USA. It read:

On November 18, 1944, at 11:30 a.m., my plane was shot down by a German antiaircraft battery. I had to bail out and successfully landed in the vicinity of Ribnica. I was slightly wounded but the townspeople helped me. They were very kind to me. Soon afterward I was captured by the Germans who kept me in Ribnica for five days. Then they took me together with my crew to Ljubljana, where I was also imprisoned. The warden as well as the guards of that large civil prison were very kind to me.

Now I would like to thank all those who helped me. At the same time I would like to show my family where I had landed and where I had been imprisoned in Ribnica and Ljubljana and, if possible, the interior of the prisons. I would be very grateful to someone who could help me do all of these things.

When I parachuted down into the area surrounding Ribnica I became acquainted with a girl who intended to get married at that time. I gave her my parachute so that she could use the material for her wedding dress. If possible, I would like to see her again and meet her family, too.

Bill Swigert, extreme right, and Swigert's family during their visit to Slovenia with a woman who helped the WWII airman.

After reading the story, the Slovenian accompanied the Americans to the town hall, which was close by. He introduced them to the president of the town assembly, Stane Kromar, who hospitably received them and invited them inside to talk. Kromar called Ing. Marjan Hočevar, who had been in the USA for several years, to come and assist them in interpreting.

While Marjan gladly accepted the invitation, Kromar also took the opportunity to telephone me and inform me of the interesting event. I arrived within the next hour along with all of my documents concerning similar cases from that area.

The visitor, William Swigert, recollected his flight.

* * * * *

On November 18, 1944, I was a navigator on a B-24 bomber on my nineteenth combat flight over Germany and its occupied territories. Our target was the Udine airport in Italy. We were flying at an altitude of 22,000 feet. We had been warned that there would be some antiaircraft protection, but it was much stronger than we had expected. This was due to the numerous new antiaircraft cannons mounted on railroad cars that the Germans had brought into the Udine area. Their fire was powerfully focused upon our 28 aircraft.

My plane was severely damaged. Only one engine was operating at full power, the remaining three on partial power. Some of the crew members were wounded, as I was, but nobody paid any attention to our wounds at that time. A gaping hole had appeared; shrapnel tore off one-half of my navigation map. We re-directed the plane southward, using elapsed time to chart our course.

Prior to leaving our air base earlier that morning, we were supplied with information regarding the location of the Partisan airstrips; however, I could not remember that particular data. We were flying over forests when we noticed two large towns ahead of us [Ribnica and Kočevje]. We were sure that there were Germans in those places, and therefore, lest we fall into their hands, we decided to bail out somewhere between those two settlements.

The Group leader, First Lieutenant R. E. Reed, ordered, "Bail out!" To tell you the truth, some of us had never bailed out with a parachute before, not even in training. Somehow, the first crewman [James Mund] got out, but I had to push the second one ["Smokey" Dunham] through the opening. It was not easy for the rest of us. Who would push me? I wondered. I was the last one to jump.

At first, everything seemed okay. It was only when I landed that I sprained my ankle. One of the crewmen landed on top of a tree and was badly hurt; the skin on his face was quite scraped. Two girls ran to me and helped me get up. I walked with much difficulty. Soon six of us gathered and went toward a barn. The landowner also rushed to it and offered us some brandy. I took it — it was useful, especially for disinfecting my crew's wounds. Meanwhile, some soldiers arrived after following our tracks while riding their bicycles [these were the local quislings from Ribnica]. Before long, an elderly priest about 80 years old arrived. He advised the soldiers to let the Germans know that we were there, or else they would level the town. It did not take very long before the Germans came. They took us to the prison in the center of the town, where we stayed for several days, and then for 12 days in the Ljubljana prison, and finally another 6 months in a German POW camp by the Baltic Sea. Before being liberated, I weighed barely 100 pounds.

* * * * *

I suggested that the American inspect the area where everything had happened. At Otavica, near Ribnica, there wasn't a barn anywhere. In its place was a new house. William scanned the surroundings for a long time before he remembered where he had bailed out; he then showed us the place where he had landed. The girls who had helped him were gone, as was the bride who got married in a wedding dress made from his parachute. But they did meet Marija Šteblaj, who lived at the edge of Ribnica. She had five brothers and a husband who were with the Partisans. She remembered the

A treasured piece of an airman's parachute, similar to that used to make a wedding dress during WWII.

event vividly. She had seen the wounded airmen and had shown one of them directions to the forest. She believed he had succeeded in escaping.

Marija had been very sorry when she saw the others being led to prison by the Germans and their collaborators. She had wished that she could have helped them.

The entire conversation was translated to the Americans. William and his wife, Jo, were moved and thanked the old woman for her concern. Then Swigert gave her a hug as if she were his own mother.

Just prior to leaving the kind villagers of Otavica, an elderly peasant woman ran to us with a small surprise for the Americans. She brought forth a large piece of a parachute that she had kept in a chest in her house. They all gathered around to gaze at the piece of nylon that 35 years ago had perhaps saved William's life.

It was while they were in Ribnica that William learned for the first time the destiny of four of the other crew members. Lieutenant Reed had landed near a ridge about 15 to 20 miles southeast of Ribnica. He buried his chute and headed due east. While walking that night he met a Partisan wagon on the road and hitched a ride to a Partisan headquarters. The Partisans were battling with some Germans over the next ridge, and after this had been concluded, they continued onwards toward a town near Metlika where they stayed overnight. The next day at 5:00 p.m. they arrived at the British mission in Metlika.

Meanwhile, Lieutenant Jerome Jares had landed about 500 yards from the aircraft, which had just crashed with a heavy explosion. Hearing a considerable amount of shooting in his vicinity, he decided to hide out until after nightfall. A German patrol came within a few feet of his hidden position within the next two hours. Later that night he struck out in a southeasterly direction, eventually coming across a barn where he expected to sleep the rest of the night. He no sooner covered himself with some hay when another person entered the barn and also stayed overnight. When he awoke the next morning, the unknown visitor was gone.

Jares found he was in a small village and singled out one house for food. The inhabitants fed him, and one of the men left to get the Partisans. Soon afterward, one of the men in the house reported that some Germans were coming, so Jares quickly left and once again hid himself in the woods. Shortly thereafter, he approached a man sawing wood and tried to make him understand that he wanted to contact the Partisans up in the hills. He was then escorted to a whole division of Partisans who were busily engaging the Germans nearby. Two days later, he arrived at the British mission in Metlika.

The following account of that memorable flight and personal experience was provided by Sergeant James Mund, who was on his thirty-third mission and who served as the nose gunner and armorer on the crew.

* * * * *

There was a slight haze over the ground as we approached Udine, but it wasn't so dense that we couldn't see through it. There were also some high cirrus cloud layers at our altitude, but they were not thick enough to obscure us from the German gunners on the ground. As we approached the target on the bomb run, I remember being a little more apprehensive about this trip than usual. There were no enemy fighters, but the first barrage of flak that came up hit one of the planes in our formation. He pulled out of the formation, but I didn't see where he had gone. The second string of bursts hit us.

I believe that we were struck about the time we dropped our bombs, but the flight engineer advised the pilot on the intercom that ten 100-pound bombs (of the original 40) hadn't released and remained in the bomb bay. Theoretically, it was the responsibility of the bombardier ("Smokey" Dunham) and the armorer to go into the bomb bay and release them manually: unscrew the shackles, kick them out, and the like. However, the bays were so cramped that there wasn't room to wear a parachute in there, and with the aircraft obviously losing altitude rapidly, the prospects of being anywhere in the damaged airplane without a chute didn't appeal to either one of us.

The decision to wear a parachute was decided immediately afterward when the order to bail out was given. When my parachute opened, I could see our plane flying away. For a few moments, nobody else jumped, and I thought for a minute that they had repaired the aircraft and were continuing homeward. But before I hit the ground, I saw another chute pop open. It turned out to be Leland Brown, our tail gunner, bailing out of the waist escape hatch. It was his first jump.

After I landed in a clearing on the side of a small mountain, I buried my chute in a snowbank and started walking southeast. I didn't know where I was, or even if we had crossed the Italian border before I jumped. Then I encountered Leland Brown. He and I walked together the rest of the day toward the plane crash site to see if there were any other survivors. We eluded two German patrols that were heading in the same direction. After three hours we looked over a small rise and spotted the wreckage — and also three German soldiers guarding it. Brown and I managed to sneak away unseen.

We followed a footpath through the woods, hoping it might lead us to a remote cabin or farmhouse where we might obtain some food. We were both armed with .45 Colt automatics and figured if we found a place sufficiently isolated we might be able to get help, regardless of whether the occupants were friendly or not.

Half an hour later I turned a bend in the path and nearly bumped into a youth who was holding what appeared to be a huge rifle pointed directly at us. It would have been foolish to try to reach for my gun, so we just raised our hands in surrender.

He asked us something in his language. I didn't understand. He whistled, never taking his eyes or his gun off of us, and several more men emerged from the bushes and the trees. I tried to speak German with only marginal success. Finally, it seemed to me, one of the men asked if we were *"Amerikanski"* — neither they nor we had any insignia — and we admitted that we were. Their leader spoke some English. He told me that he had been trained by the British as a commando and that he and his patrol were there to dynamite a railroad the Germans used to ship troops and supplies to their garrisons in Yugoslavia.

We all waited until darkness and then proceeded to the railroad tracks where they planted the explosives. We then retreated back up the mountain and waited. It was completely dark — maybe midnight — when we first heard a train puffing up the valley. Then we could see the glow of its firebox.

Suddenly, the entire valley lit up; it seemed almost as bright as day, and the train was no more. The patrol then gathered their things, and we left in a hurry. I remember helping carry some of their equipment.

Later that night we slept in the remains of a small town (Metlika?) that had been destroyed in some old battle. The following day the patrol led us to a farmhouse. In the excavated basement of the house were nearly two dozen Allied soldiers and airmen, including my pilot, Bob Reed, and copilot, Jerry Jares, who had arrived the night before. The next day a British C-47 was expected to land in the field adjacent to the house with supplies for the Partisans and then to fly us back to Italy. It was then that I offered one member of this gutsy Partisan patrol my Colt automatic as a thank-you for all their help. It was all I had of any value that I could offer as a gift, and since I apparently would be flying back to Italy the next day, I thought I wouldn't need it any more. I don't remember any of their names.

Unfortunately, it snowed that night, and the plane couldn't land without leaving tracks and exposing the farmhouse as a haven for escapees. Therefore, a group of about 18 of us left, including Reed, Jares, Brown, and myself. Some of the others were injured and couldn't manage the long walk, so the Partisans agreed that they could stay and would be protected to the best of their ability. We walked for more than three weeks, sometimes day and night. One day we rode in a truck that the Partisans had "liberated" from the Germans.

We were finally guided to the seaport town of Zadar, where a British cruiser was anchored in the harbor. A small boat picked us up, and we spent the night on the cruiser. The next day we transferred to a British destroyer that returned us to Italy.

* * * * *

The following account is from Rafko Krošelj, the Partisan youth who saw five parachutists from Reed's crew and who first encountered Sergeants Mund and Brown in the woods.

* * * * *

Three of my family joined the Partisans. After a course in explosives, I joined a Partisan demolition battalion. By laying mines we were destroying railroads, roads, bridges, strongholds, vehicles, and the like. We did not want the enemy to have a moment's rest and wanted him to be aware of us, to strike him with terror and awe-inspiring unpredictable destructive actions. In the middle of November a group in our battalion was given an order to destroy a part of the railroad line between Kočevje and Ribnica. Heavily loaded with equipment, we set out and reached our appointed place after a 12-mile walk.

Since it was still daylight and close to an enemy stronghold, we decided to wait in a nearby woods until darkness. We prepared everything so that, at the right moment, we could accomplish the entrusted task in the quickest and best possible way.

But in the next few minutes something occurred that temporarily diverted us. After the war I recollected that event several times and decided to document everything in detail lest it be forgotten. It was due to our immediate action that we saved some Allied airmen who would otherwise have fallen into enemy hands.

I was on sentry duty when a large aircraft attracted my attention as it flew over our post at an unusually low altitude. I immediately informed our leader. Shortly after that I again caught sight of the aircraft. It flew even lower than before and one wing was low. A moment later, totally out of control, the plane crashed. Looking up I saw some airmen parachuting toward us.

At first we sighted five airmen; however, one of them drifted toward Kočevje and vanished from sight, while four of them landed some distance from us in the woods. We rushed in their direction to reach them as soon as possible and save them. We were quite sure that they were Allied airmen. We searched the area for a long time before we found them. I could imagine their tension and anxiety lest they should be captured by the Germans, so we were not surprised in the least when we saw two airmen behind a fir tree. They hesitated to fire at us since our clothes were different from the expected German uniforms. We had civilian clothes on, which was also suspicious, for they did not know if we were Partisans or collaborators. It wasn't easy for us to make ourselves understood that we wanted to rescue them and bring them to safety. Their suspicions were finally assuaged when they saw that our leader had a Partisan uniform and a proper cap with a red star. We had difficulty trying to speak to each other. We did not know English, so we somehow made ourselves understood by using some German.

We greeted each other warmly and shook hands. The airmen told us, in very poor German, that they had been hit over Udine, Italy, as they were on their way back to their base. One crew member had already been shot in the plane while the others had drifted far away and had landed in an enemy outpost.

They offered us cigarettes, which were a great treat for us, but I was a non-smoker, so they gave me some chocolate. I had nearly forgotten what it tasted like. After I explained the plan that we had in mind, they were immediately enthusiastic. I was the youngest in the group — only 15 years old — not strong and without warm clothing. Therefore, one of the airmen volunteered to carry my pickax. We then continued toward our planned destination.

The Americans expressed interest in our mine-laying operation. They watched as we placed several wooden boxes on the road. Each box contained 20 pounds of explosives, which we camouflaged; then we obliterated any

Partisans lying in ambush.

surrounding ground tracks. We normally observed the results of our work while hiding from a distant vantage point in order to benefit from the experience, but on this occasion we decided to forego the viewing in order to minimize the risk and danger to our rescued airmen. We were already far from the site when we heard the resultant explosion a short time later; then we knew that our task had been successful.

The Americans continued to carry our pickaxes more than 15 miles despite the fact that they could not walk without great difficulty due to wearing poorly fitting flying boots, which were unsuitable for walking any distance. We eventually stopped for a rest at Žužemberk, then continued walking again for a few hours.

Finally we came to a farm. The peasants prepared a hasty pudding and milk for us. We ate it all as if it were the most delicious meal we had ever eaten, but the Americans did not even touch it. They just drank some milk. We all could have slept much longer but were awakened to continue our walk. We eventually reached our unit and reported our accomplishments to our commander, leaving the Americans with him.

One of the airmen turned to us and thanked us for bringing them to safety. In remembrance of the occasion, he left us his .45 Colt automatic pistol.

As soon as they had rested and refreshed themselves, they were escorted to the village of Otok in Bela Krajina by the couriers of the XV Division.

After the war I received copies of the document "Allied Airmen and

Prisoners of War Rescued by the Slovene Partisans," published by the Research Institute Ljubljana in 1946, proof that the Americans returned safely to the USA and their families.

*　*　*　*　*

Rafko Krošelj has not forgotten the American who unselfishly helped him, a weak and starving youth, by carrying his pickax. He has prepared a handmade gift to be given to the American but has never had the chance to present it to him.

From the Official Record

On November 18, 1944, at 0730, 30 aircraft of the 460th Bomb Group based near Spinazzola, Italy, were dispatched to bomb the Udine Airdrome in northern Italy. The Group was led by Group Commanding Officer Colonel John M. Price. Two of the aircraft had to turn back with engine trouble after jettisoning 80 bombs in the Adriatic Sea. Of the remaining 28, two were lost and 11 were damaged in the attack. The crew of one of the two lost aircraft were Lieutenant Robert E. Reed (pilot), Lieutenant Jerome Jares (copilot), Lieutenant William Swigert (navigator), Lieutenant Forest Dunham (bombardier), Sergeant John Corley (flight engineer), and gunners Sergeant Leland Brown, Sergeant Frank Coyle, Sergeant William Franklin, Sergeant James Mund, and Sergeant Adrian Patton.

During the flight over the target area, flak severely damaged engines number 1 and number 3, which were then feathered. Only half-power was available on the remaining two engines as they attempted to head back down the Yugoslavian coastline. The gunners threw all of the ammunition overboard in order to make the aircraft lighter. However, they had lost so much altitude that they couldn't climb over the mountain range just south of Ljubljana, Yugoslavia. Consequently, the crew members started to bail out south of the town of Ribnica. All of the crew bailed out and all chutes opened. Sergeants Mund and Brown were the first to bail out.

Four of the crew, Reed, Jares, Mund, and Brown, were rescued by the Partisans and reunited a few days later in Metlika; the rest of the crew had either been captured or killed. They left on Thursday, November 23, and walked in short marches until Sunday, November 26, when the group was held up for three days due to active German patrols in the area. They finally went through the German lines on November 29 and arrived in Pisarovina, approximately 30 miles south of Zagreb, on November 30. They arrived at Mission "Fungus" on Saturday, December 2, where they stayed until the following Thursday. They left that evening by truck. After many stops and after passing close to the collaborating Ustashi troops, they arrived at

Obrovazzo, approximately 20 miles east of Zadar, on Saturday night. The next day, after an all-day ride, they arrived at Zadar and boarded a British light cruiser. Two days later they transferred to a British destroyer and arrived at Bari on Thursday, December 14, 1944.

Chapter 15

Downed in Planica

In November 1944, the upper Sava valley was the scene of wartime activity as hundreds and hundreds of Allied aircraft flew over it almost daily. They bombed ammunition dumps, railway junctions, bridges, and military installations in Villach and Klagenfurt. Death and destruction were left behind them before they returned along the same route. Although Hitler's military forces were resisting fiercely, it was well known that their efforts only prolonged their eventual defeat. Consequently, the Allied air forces received their share of casualties.

On November 22, one of the aircraft was lagging behind its formation, trailing thick, black smoke. It had lost too much altitude to fly over the Julian Alps and crashed in the Kotovo saddle beneath the face of Mount Jalovec (the remains can still be seen). The explosion resulting from the impact echoed from Planica. The inhabitants of the town in the beautiful Tamar valley, frightened observers of the dreadful event, could provide no assistance as the Germans were already rushing to the scene.

Alojz Ples, from Rateče, was 14 years old at the time and a member of the Young Partisans organization in the district. He remembered the event and stated:

> Just before the airplane crashed we saw parachutes opening high up in the sky. The wind blew the airmen toward Kranska Gora and Gozd Martuljek, where there were strong detachments of the occupation forces. I heard a lot of shooting. The Nazis probably killed some of the Americans while they were still in the air, and they immediately shot those they caught behind what is now Rozman's home and simply buried them in a dung heap. [After the

The area of the plane crash site in the Julian Alps near the Tamar valley.

war, the bodies were exhumed and buried in a common grave in Belgrade.] However, the strong wind blew one of them to Tamar. He probably survived.

He did survive. He landed behind the hill and remained hidden in the snow by his white parachute.

There was a secluded gatekeeper's house for the railroad crossing between the Rateče and Podgorn stations. It was not in service. Only Uršula Zima with her 11-year-old son, Lojze, and 5-year-old daughter, Marija, lived there. She had stepped out of her house on that day and had watched the airmen parachuting. Her wish that she might be able to help them was soon to be fulfilled.

I interviewed Uršula Zima at her home in Gozd Martuljek and asked her to describe the events.

* * * * *

I saw the parachutists as they bailed out and was afraid that they would run into trouble. There were Germans everywhere, and there was little hope that anyone would survive. There was a half-meter of snow on the ground already, and two days later it started to snow again. By that time we had almost

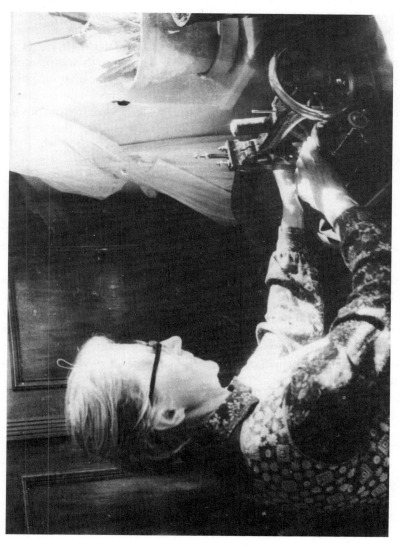

Uršula Zima of Gozd Martuljek, who hid David Holdsworth from the Nazis.

forgotten about the plane. I left the gatekeeper's house to feed the livestock —
it was approaching nightfall — when all of a sudden I saw the figure of a man
coming toward me. He stopped in front of me and said, *"Amerikano,
Amerikano,"* making signs to show me that he was hungry. I was frightened; I
didn't know who he was. He might have been a Nazi in disguise trying to trap
me — or, if he really was an American, there might be a German patrol
somewhere nearby. But I decided to help him anyway. I pushed him into the
kitchen and gave him some hot water and something to eat. He must have been
very hungry, for he ate everything that I brought to him.

Since we could not understand each other, I tried to communicate with him
by means of drawings and gestures. When he saw the map, he took out his own
in order to determine his position. Meanwhile I went out again and covered all
of the tracks in the new snow. When I came back into the kitchen I found him
sitting on a box used for storing firewood. The warmth was making him
sleepy, but he did not give in to sleep. He kept watching the map and pointed to
Italy all the time. He pointed to Rome saying "choo, choo, choo." His
intention was to travel to Italy by train. I tried to dissuade him from this idea —
the Germans would track him and his destiny would be the same as his
comrades'.

When he heard the train at the station, he jumped out of the gatekeeper's
house, went to the station, and boarded. I do not know what happened to him
in the next few hours. Soon after the last train for the day had arrived at the
station, someone banged on my door. It was the airman, and he was very
angry. I stepped outside to see if there were any other tracks leading from the
station to my house, but there were none but his. I later learned the
circumstances that had led him to come back to the gatekeeper's house.

After wandering a bit, the airman had reached the railway station in Radeče
and boarded the evening train. He thought he was going to the Italian border
but learned that it was going to the Austrian border at Jesenice. As soon as the
train started to move, one of our people in the resistance must have noticed
him. As there were Germans aboard inspecting all of the documents, he
decided to push the airman off at a spot where the snow was so deep that he
couldn't hurt himself.

* * * * *

So the American was back in the kitchen, but his hostess was very
concerned. She realized that the matter was getting more and more dangerous.

* * * * *

At that time my son, Lozje, was quite a big boy and a member of the Young

Partisans organization. He suggested that we prepare a hiding place for the American in the woods until the Partisans returned. Instead I decided to dig a hole for him in the barn. After that, I went to bed. But I didn't sleep at all that night since I was worried and expected the police would knock on my door as they were making their rounds. Luckily, nothing like that happened.

* * * * *

Meanwhile, the Germans did not rest. They kept inquiring and looking for the parachutists. It was nearly dawn when Uršula went to Medja in the neighboring village of Podkoren and asked him to inform the Partisans.

* * * * *

The very next day they knocked on my door. I knew the Partisans and led them through the first room, which was empty, and then to the American in the barn. In the middle of the barn stood the short, fair-haired young man. He was at a loss for words and looked worried, but when he saw the Partisans in their uniforms with a red star on their caps, he jumped up and down for joy and kept repeating, "*ami* Partisan, *ami* Partisan." But there was no time for talking; they just shook hands. It was nearly daylight, so they had to hurry before sunup to cross a dangerous area that afforded no sheltering screen. As we parted, we said we hoped to see one another again after we were freed, but he never came back.

* * * * *

Boris Ojcel, the Partisan who helped the American return to liberated territory, told me what he knew about the airman's rescue.

* * * * *

At that time I was a courier in the Intelligence Center SPIK. We had a cave in the vicinity of the Cimperski saddle. I remember the courier Tone Hočever rushing in and shouting, "Invasion! Invasion!" He had noticed several parachutes high up in the sky above us. "Don't be daft; there's no invasion!" I said to him, because the explosion we heard was from the crashed plane.

We carefully noted the direction of the descending parachutists. One of them was swinging above the fir trees very close to our bunkered cave. We all agreed at once that we must get that one. At that moment we heard shooting in the distance. It was the Germans shooting at the airmen as the wind drifted

Boris Ojcel, at right, was 16 years old when he first inspected the site where the airman had landed.

their chutes toward Kranska Gora and Podkoren.

We formed two groups to at least try to rescue the one airman. There wasn't a chance for the rest of them. There were five of us: Ivan Pristavec, Franc Vandot, Tone Hočever, Franc Godec (called Adrijan), and me. We searched the entire area of Vitranc in deep snow, but there was no trace of the airman. However, we knew that he must be somewhere in the surrounding countryside.

We then had to stop our search. In the Mala Pišnica valley far below us we had previously noticed a German patrol that also sought the American with different intentions from ours. Although we had only two rifles and a machine gun, we decided to attack the Germans on their way back to Pišnica.

We positioned ourselves and took the enemy by surprise. The Germans returned our fire. It was very possible that the downed airman was between the two lines of fire.

It soon got dark. The Germans returned to their base, and we retreated to our bunker. We were aware that we couldn't stay there any longer, for the Germans would return the next day in greater numbers. We split up early in the morning and rejoined other groups in the area. Adrijan and I went to Godevar's house. Soon afterward we learned that the American was hiding in the gatekeeper's house.

When Adrijan and I became responsible for the American, he was still sure that he was going to Italy. Placing the airman in the middle, we crawled for a while along the railroad tracks till we reached a road bordered by high banks of snow. Adrijan offered the American his big Colt, a pistol with three bullets — just in case. David — that was the American's name — obviously satisfied, stuck it in his belt. When we were sure that nobody was near the road, we rolled over the snow bank and headed toward the juntion with the bridge across the Sava River at the base of Srednji Vrh.

We stopped and listened. There seemed to be something wrong. We had a strange feeling. Sure enough, our foreboding didn't deceive us, for we noticed a small flame a moment later. One of the Germans who was waiting in ambush could not resist lighting a cigarette. It had probably saved our lives.

Because of that unexpected situation, we had to make a large detour so that we could climb Srednji Vrh from the other side to reach a Partisan post above the village. We arrived at our destination and turned the American over to the leader of the Intelligence post. Although he didn't show it, we knew our guest was totally exhausted. It was understandable, since his shoes were not suitable for walking in deep snow.

With the aid of an interpreter, it was explained to David that it would take him a long time to cover four different regions in Slovenia before reaching Bela Krajina from where he could board a military plane and fly back to Italy.

* * * * *

According to "Allied Airmen and Prisoners of War Rescued by the Slovene Partisans," it is evident that David Holdsworth's evasion after November 25, 1944, was successful. A month later he reached the airstrip at Bela Krajina and boarded the plane to Italy on December 27. Seven days later he celebrated his nineteenth birthday with his Air Force unit in Southern Italy.

I tried very hard to locate David to determine if any others in the crew had survived. It was years before I succeeded in obtaining his address, which had changed over the intervening years. Finally, I received the following letter from Alaska:

20 May 79
Copenhagen

Gentlemen,

Just a short note in answer to your kind letter dated 29 March. I have been working for Japan Airlines as a captain for more than 10 years now. I started as a captain on Boeing 727 aircraft and went on with the DC-8 and have been on the Boeing 747 now for 5 years. I am now in Copenhagen (in a terrible hotel). Tomorrow I fly to Zurich and back to Copenhagen and then to Paris and then back home over the North Pole to Anchorage.

I will write a more detailed letter later when I review my WW II records. I can tell you now that I was a gunner on a B-24 named "BUGS BUNNY" when we were hit by 88mm flak during a bomb run over Munich. I first met the Partisans outside of a small [Austrian] village called Villach. Two men came to get me named Andre and Boris [Franc Godec ("Adrijan") and Boris Ojcel ("Mirko")]. Andre was an older gentleman and Boris looked to be a lad of 12-14 years. He had a pistol almost as big as he was. From then on I was relayed to other underground guides and was finally taken to (I believe) the Yugoslav village of Chernomel [Černomelj, a town in southern Slovenia] where I stayed with several other escaping airmen and troops (British, American, Russian, etc.) for several days before we were picked up by a C-47 "Dakota" and flown back to Bari in Italy. It was quite a trip and I was indeed fortunate that I was contacted by the Partisans first and not the Germans!

I went through pilot training in 1948. Flew B-29's in the Korean conflict, in 1953 went to test pilot school and spent my last 13 years in the Air Force as a test pilot. I retired from the Air Force in 1966, spent 2-5 years with Boeing as a test pilot before going to Japan Airlines.

Longer more detailed letter follows.

Regards,

Dave Holdsworth

P.S. There are some photos of the Liberator "BUGS BUNNY" available.

Unfortunately, the letter that should have followed the one dated 20 May 1979 never came.

Chapter 16

I Have Kissed the Soil
on the Isle of Vis

Among the Allied Air Forces pilots who made a forced landing on liberated Yugoslav territory during World War II was George McGovern, who later became a United States senator and a presidential candidate. He was only 22 years old when he became captain of a flight of B-24 Liberator four-engined heavy bombers.

On July 24, 1979, I wrote to him, taking the liberty of asking him to describe his experiences that resulted in his forced landing on Vis, a small island in the Adriatic Sea off the coast of Yugoslavia. On September 10, 1979, I received his reply.

* * * * *

It was December 8, 1944. That day's mission was an air raid upon the Skoda factories in Pilsen in the German-occupied territory of Czechoslovakia. These factories were producing all kinds of arms for Hitler's Germany. We took off from our base in Cerignola, Italy, joined our formation, and, at 25,000 feet, flew over the Alps, which were overcast with clouds. We soon passed the Alps and the cloud cover and proceeded to the target area in good weather. About an hour before we reached our target, I noticed that the number 2 engine was losing oil pressure. When that engine failed, I increased power on the remaining three engines in order to keep up with the rest of our formation. When we arrived at our target an hour later, the need for additional power had caused damage to the number 3 engine. Oil pressure was diminishing so rapidly that we could not "feather" the propeller, which continued windmill-

George McGovern.

ing, causing the aircraft to slow down. We immediately descended to leave the formation and release the bombs. At that point we were about 600 miles from our base in Italy.

When we lost altitude, our navigator, Sim Adams, directed the plane to the east toward Yugoslavia where we knew that only a small number of antiaircraft guns were located. When we finally reached the Adriatic coast, our altitude was barely 600 feet. In order to unburden the aircraft, I ordered the crew to jettison all equipment not required to sustain flight: ammunition, machine guns, oxygen reservoirs, everything that could possibly be removed.

At that moment, Adams informed me that the island of Vis was below us. The British had built a short landing strip there for their Spitfire fighters. It was only 2,000 feet long — far too short for landing a B-24 bomber — but there was no other choice. When we made a circle of the island we noticed wreckages of other planes that had tried but failed; their remains were piled up at the end of the runway. When we finally touched down, both Bill Rounds, the copilot, and I pushed the brake pedals with all our might. The plane stopped! In no time at all the crew jumped out of the plane and literally kissed the soil. The Partisans sent a message to our base in Italy that we had landed safely, and a C-47 (DC-3) was dispatched to Vis to return us to our base.

Our last combat flight was successfully completed before the end of the war. The aim of that last mission was an air raid upon a crucially important railway junction in Linz, Austria, so that we could prevent the movement of the rest of the German forces. That was also one of our most daring actions. Our old B-24 was hit and damaged by over a hundred pieces of antiaircraft shrapnel. Worst of all, one of our gunners, Bill Ashlock, was hit and painfully wounded. But it was also the end of the war.

The youngsters who enlisted in the Army Air Forces became mature men. In June 1945, I flew the crew from Europe back to the USA. My thoughts were turned from the war toward peace.

* * * * *

In 1977 George McGovern visited Vis. As he walked around the area that once had been a Partisan airport, he said, "I owe my life to this soil."

A vineyard currently occupies the site of the earlier Partisan airstrip. "I will visit this island once more with my family," said McGovern at parting. "It would be a real blessing if vineyards were planted on all military airfields."

Anton Sever was working as a mechanic in a Partisan squadron when George McGovern made his forced landing on Vis. As a witness to that event, he relates:

> It was a dry and cold winter day. The sun was already low in the sky and shone dimly through the delicate and feathery-looking cirrus clouds.
>
> Then the air above the island vibrated as if a volcano had erupted. Several thousand meters above us, nearly up to the white veil of clouds, we could see hundreds of bombers flying towards the coast en route to the enemy.

Anton stopped working for a while to gaze at the tiny aircraft, which appeared as dots emitting vapor trails. If only they would come back safely, he thought to himself as he resumed his work.

> We had been waiting for hours for the planes to return. The sun had started to set when the first flock of aircraft appeared. Disorderly and scattered formations overflew Vis in the direction of Italy. There were a lot of war-damaged planes among them; black smoke trailed from some and there were many stragglers. Far behind the initial group trailed a B-24 with one wing low and only two engines operational. A good portion of its right wing was also missing.

Anton was busy dismantling a damaged plane at the edge of the airport. Suddenly his attention was attracted by the close sound of laboring engines. A lone Liberator overflew the airport very low, and it sounded as if only one engine was functioning. It continued to fly toward the sea, appearing as if the crew had decided to land on the water, for landing a large, damaged airplane with only one of the four engines working would have been suicide on such a small airport.

But the bomber circled once more, very gently, in a large arc until it again was headed in the direction of the landing strip. It lowered its wheels and continued at full throttle toward a risky landing. It seemed like a miracle that it could remain in the air; then it finally managed to touch down at the edge of the steel-matted strip. Squealing brakes pierced Anton's ears as the aircraft rumbled towards him and the wrecked planes at the far end of the strip.

At that point, Anton breathlessly watched and wondered: What if the plane skids at that speed and catches fire? Perhaps there are some wounded on board who are unable to move? What if the brakes don't hold? He felt that something had to be done, and quickly.

He signaled the pilot to remain in the center of the strip almost to the end, at which time he motioned the pilot to make a sharp turn toward some level ground alongside the rocks and wrecked planes. The brakes squealed for the last time as the bomber turned off from the runway and stopped right in front of him.

The engine made one last gasp as its propeller continued to wind down; it finally stopped in silence. Meanwhile, the crewmen jumped out of the bomber. For a moment they stood still; then they lifted their commander above their heads and carried him towards the front of the plane. There the pilot knelt down and kissed the soil that, from the verge of despair, had brought the crew to life again. George McGovern got up and shook Anton Sever's hand vigorously, embraced him, and, deeply touched, thanked him for his assistance.

"Thank you, friend," he breathed with gratitude. It was only then that he noticed that the mechanic had an English overall with RAF insignia on it and a cap with a red star.

"What are you doing here?" he asked him, still holding him by the shoulders.

"I'm a Partisan squadron aircraft mechanic, Section B."

"Good boy!" praised McGovern, shaking his hand once more.

As McGovern was parting the next day, Anton presented him with a star — in remembrance of the Partisan squadron on the island of Vis.

Anica Kunstek, who helped the airmen evade the enemy troops and collaborators.

Chapter 17

Bail Out at Dolenjska

Approximately 25 miles east of Ljubljana, Slovenia, a B-24 Liberator from the 455th Bomb Group was shot down on December 20, 1944. Nine members of the crew bailed out and were rescued by the Partisans. Five days later they were 30 miles due south in Bela Krajina waiting for an airplane to fly them back to their base in Bari, Italy.

As the parachutists descended into the area known as Dolenjska, their thoughts were not on the beautiful landscape but on how to survive. Those young airmen, aged 18 to 26, were lucky because the wind was drifting them toward the Mirna valley, which was under the control of a Partisan army.

No sooner had the aircraft crashed than the airmen found themselves in the trees amidst vineyards. They quickly removed their chutes and waited for people to arrive and help them.

Their waiting was not in vain. The villagers who had spotted the stricken aircraft and noted its direction when it crashed quickly set off toward the parachutists' landing site. But besides the Allied sympathizers responding to their aid were local collaborators with other intentions. Anica Kunstek Novak recalls the event quite well.

* * * * *

During the war we lived in Zavrh, near Trebnje. Our house was at the top of a hill, and we had a beautiful view in all directions. My mother and I lived there alone. At the time one of my sisters was with the Partisans and the other was in the concentration camp in Ravensbruck. I remember it was a few days before Christmas 1944 when a large formation of planes flew over our house. We always looked forward to hearing the Allied planes since they projected hope that the end of the war was drawing closer.

This time we stepped outside to watch them. We suddenly noticed one of the aircraft flying lower than the rest. It ascended slightly and then crashed in the village of Rihpovec, some two miles away.

Later I noticed that the plane had crashed through a vineyard cottage and caught fire. All ten crew members had previously bailed out. Six of them landed in the vicinity of Mirna, and the remaining four came down over Rihpovec. Unfortunately, one of the latter group landed on top of the burning airplane. After I saw where the three others had landed, I ran into the house and related to the two Partisans inside what had happened. Simultaneously a group of the collaborators also had set out from their outpost to apprehend the Americans. We ran as fast as we could and arrived at the farm where they had taken shelter. Initially we could not make them understand that we wanted to lead them to safety before the collaborators from Sv. Anna arrived. Since there was no time left to persuade them, the two armed Partisans with me ordered them to follow us into the nearby woods. None of us spoke anything but Slovene, and they only spoke English. Although the Americans came with us, they still did not understand that we wanted to save them. On the way they made signs as if we were going to shoot them.

We made our first stop at the top of Mount Kraljevac, arriving out of breath and near the end of our destination (the Americans thought it was the end). You can imagine their relief when the word "Tito" finally cleared the situation. We sat down in the woods, and one of them took out a special map — it was printed on silk cloth — and located our present position and where the airplane had crashed. We continued to travel together for a short while, and then our ways parted at Stara Gora. The two Partisans escorted them on quite a long march till they finally arrived at a fairly large Partisan unit. You can imagine their happiness when they found the other six surviving crew members there.

*   *   *   *   *

Anica remembered some of the details of that first meeting. All three airmen were very young. Two were tall and dark while the other was shorter and blond. Throughout the trek she had supported one of the airmen who had been injured while landing. When they parted, the airman gave her a monographed silk handkerchief and a notebook in which there were several addresses. He also gave her a big signet ring from his finger and reluctantly took it back after she made signs that it was much too big for her.

Anica went back home feeling happy that she had helped to bring the airmen to safety in the nick of time. As soon as the collaboration forces learned about the rescue operation, they began shooting at Anica's house with large-caliber guns. This continued sporadically over the next two months to the point where she and her mother could not sleep in the house during this period.

Anica is retired now and lives in a suburb of Ljubljana. She remembers that Americans who were rescued in those times tried to contact the people who had helped them through the Red Cross, but in the meantime she has lost all of the things that they gave her as souvenirs when they parted.

However, on April 24, 1986, a letter was received by *Rodna Gruda*, a Slovene magazine published monthly in Ljubljana, Yugoslavia, and distributed worldwide:

> . . . We flew B-24's (heavy bombardment) which were manned by 10-man crews and were officially attached on November 24, 1944 to the 455th Bomb Group, 741st Bomb Squadron, stationed in Cerignola, Italy. We flew practice missions until December 7th. We flew our first credited mission to Bleckhammer (Odertal) Germany — an oil refinery — on December 17th. Our second mission was to Pilsen, Czechoslovakia on December 20, 1944. We were assigned to an old B-24 that was one of the few that came back from the Ploesti, Roumania oil field raid. Before reaching the target, we had trouble with the #1 engine and because we had no reserve standpipe of oil, when the oil pressure was lost we were unable to feather the propeller. Consequently, the plane became uncontrollable. Lt. Bone, the first pilot, ordered us to bail out (our crew's first pilot, Lt. Bathman, was flying copilot for the first five missions as was the standard practice). We knew we were in enemy territory at the foothills of the Alps. We jumped at 14,000 feet.
>
> After my 'chute opened I could not see the ground, only the peaks sticking through the overcast. The plane just spun in and disappeared into the overcast. I made a safe landing on the side of a hill and saw three or four men running toward me. They stopped after seeing that I was armed, and one held out his hand and said "me Partisan." I was never happier in my life. He took me to his home for sausage and spirits whereupon I gave his wife my 'chute and passed around cigarettes.
>
> A well-dressed man came to the house and insisted that I come with him, which I did, and was reunited with my navigator, Lt. Julius Caeser Phillips. They took us to where the plane had crashed and on the way we passed some women carrying "chaff" (tinfoil) which we had tossed out of the airplane during the course of the mission to confuse the enemy radar. The plane had hit a building or barn and the Lt. and I helped to roll some large barrels away from the fire which was still burning with ammunition exploding from

Partisans and rescued American airmen (center) pose in temporary liberated territory.

the turret guns. A couple of men got very agitated and wanted to get us away and we went to 'Mirna' where we joined members of the Partisan army and met the rest of our crew — about six hours after our jump. All were present except one, first pilot Lt. Bathman, who we later heard was captured. Our acting first pilot, Lt. Bone, fractured his ankle, but outside of that there were no other casualties. We all got very drunk on schnapps and wine that night as we knew we were with the Partisan army and felt halfway secure for the first time. We started out walking in a column about 4 p.m. December 21. We encountered machine-gun fire and flares about 10 p.m. and retraced our route back toward Mirna until 4 a.m. We returned to within 4 miles of Mirna and stopped for the day because of enemy activity ahead of us. We began walking once more at 4 p.m. and walked all night, arriving at Žužemberg about 9 a.m. We continued on to Črnomelj, arriving at midnight and spent the rest of the night there. We commenced walking to a mission at 1 p.m., arriving . . . at 3 a.m. on December 24th. Approximately 20 escapees were also gathered there. A British C-47 landed at the airstrip . . . and we took off shortly thereafter.

We arrived at Foggia, Italy on December 27th. After debriefing, delousing, etc. we returned to our airbase and flew 20 more missions until the war ended. We then flew our plane back home via North Africa, Dakar, Brazil, British Guyana [*sic*], Porto Rico [*sic*], and then Hamilton Field, Georgia.

Sorry for the delay in writing you. If you have any questions, please write me. . . .

                                                  Sincerely,
                                                  Allan M. Dallian

Chapter 18

Mr. Ashley's Christmas Feast

Dr. Albin Stritar, a specialist in biochemistry and a professor at the Biotechnical Faculty in Ljubljana, met James Ashley while visiting the USA in 1959. While they were discussing various subjects, including World War II, James Ashley mentioned his experience in occupied Slovenia during that period. He didn't know where the event took place but remembered that it had occurred on December 25, 1944.

James Ashley visited Yugoslavia for the first time after the war in 1984, partially on a business trip but also as a tourist. Despite his scarce knowledge of where he was during the 1944 episode, he held onto some hope that he might locate the site of his landing. When he returned to the USA, he described his impressions and experiences of his trip in a newspaper article published in the *Newport News Times Herald* on May 8, 1985, under the headline "Anniversary Visit Revives World War II Memories." The article stated:

> . . . The landing was easier this time. As the Yugoslav Airline (JAT) DC-10 turned to make the final approach to Ljubljana Airfield in Yugoslavia, the undercast fortunately had dissipated and we saw the rolling foothills of the Julian Alps stretched out from the eastern flank of the mountains.

> My thoughts turned to my first view of the area on Christmas Day, 1944, on a return trip from bombing (with the 483rd BG) an oil refinery at Brux, Czechoslovakia [when] the crew of my B-17 was forced to bail out over Slovenia. That day was clear and crisp and, from an initial height of 12,000 feet, I felt suspended in mid-air with a wide view of the countryside.

The low mountains were singular to me, and it appeared as if a village was on top of almost every hill.

Since this was my first adventure in parachuting, I became preoccupied with the landing problem as the earth rapidly approached. Good fortune brought me down in an open field a few hundred feet from a farmhouse.

By the time I gathered up the parachute, a man who appeared unarmed was approaching. He beckoned me to follow him to his home.

His family was having afternoon tea and they offered me a Christmas cake [*potica,* dough with a honey and nut filling found only in Slovenia] and wine, which I accepted.

Apparently a messenger had been sent out, for soon after an English-speaking man appeared who explained that the area was under the control of the Chetniks and I and any others were in safe hands.

This I believed, as no weapon had been pointed at me and I was not asked to relinquish my pistol, obvious in its shoulder holster.

I passed out cigarettes and noticed the ladies were interested in the parachute, which I happily gave to them. Within a half hour, another crewman was brought in. I was most happy to see him, a fellow Virginian, as he was the last person to leave the plane, right behind me.

While enjoying Slovenian hospitality there was no time to reflect on the resistance movement. Our base intelligence was that the Chetniks were German collaborators [but apparently this was wrong, at least in our situation]. Fortune had apparently brought us to the wrong group. I and some members of my B-17 crew spent a month with the Chetniks, constantly on the move. But despite our rescue by them, the Germans later caught us under mysterious circumstances. In spite of that we were thankful that the Ustashi, deadly Fascist terrorists, had not captured us as we probably would have been killed.

My return trip proved Yugoslavia to be the same beautiful country, and one that can be enjoyed under the best of circumstances.

People with whom we talked were extremely proud of the accomplishments made in the last 40 years. They have a fierce patriotism and love of their country. We found that the younger people spoke English well and would initiate conversation whenever an opportunity arose.

Although we found the same friendly people, the country has

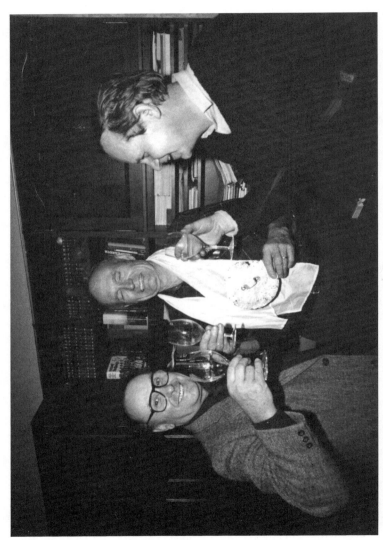

L. to r.: Dr. Albin Stritar, pilot James Ashley with a piece of his parachute around his neck (given to him in remembrance of his visit 42 years after the WWII event), and Tone Podgoršek.

changed drastically. Tourism is the biggest industry in Yugoslavia. Some 23 million people live there and about that many visitors arrive each year.

The kind of small farms I saw as a soldier are still there, but many of these now have tractors and other modern equipment. Modern transportation helps eliminate the traditional isolation of the people. People come out of the mountains to work in nearby cities and still manage to carry on small farming operations. We found Slovenes working in Montenegro and Bosnians in Slovenia.

Toward the end of 1986 James Ashley paid his second visit to Slovenia. This time he went to Ljubljana to see his acquaintance Albin Stritar. He was very much interested in finding some trace of the events that occurred almost 42 years before. Ashley mentioned three clues that might resolve the mystery: First, they had landed near the Austrian border; second, he had eaten hard maize-mush; and third, the place was called Leskovec.

James found the right person to consult: Anton Podgoršek, Stritar's son-in-law, volunteered to research the facts and learn the true story. He called the hobby OPERATION LESKOVEC.

Anton made a thorough review of the new atlas of Slovenia and found that there were no less than 17 places named Leskovec. With a team consisting of James and Beatrice Ashley, Anton Podgoršek, and his son Marko, they decided to split the work load. Using the additional clues of the Austrian border and maize-mush, they reduced the list to the Primorsko and Gorenjska areas.

While visiting an inn, they learned that there was a place called Leskovec that was not on the map and located just 10 kilometers from there. Hospitable Angelca Virnik, a member of the National Liberation Front (Partisans), did her best to make the guests feel comfortable, but she was sure that the lead was a dead end. As far as she knew, no airplane had crashed in that vicinity during the war.

They tried other places named Leskovec. They drove to Selska and Poljanska valleys where there were two places by that name. They arrived at a hamlet named Leskovec at Stari Vrh. An 80-year-old witness to the war assured them that nothing involving airplanes occurred in that area. Others confirmed this information. They finally drove on past Gorjne and Spodnje Novake above Cerkno and called on the Bevks and Kendas, who recalled that two airmen parachuted in the vicinity, but one of the Americans was wounded and taken to the Pranja hospital, so this lead was also a dead one.

When they arrived at Cerkno, they learned that there were no Chetniks in the area during the war, thereby squashing another lead. Then they set out for the village of Leskovec in Stara Oselica above Sovodnje — but that also proved to be a false lead. Finally, they decided to drive to Dolenjska, in southern Slovenia, to the village of Leskovec, eight kilometers from Višnja Gora. It was about a hundred meters' distance to the German border with Italy during the war and near the town of Grusuplje.

However, they then discovered that the maize-mush had led them astray. They do not eat maize-mush (*polenta*) in Dolenjska; in this area they eat boiled buckwheat wheat-mush (*žganci*). And that was what our American did not know; he failed to recognize the difference between the two dishes.

James got out of the car and scanned the surrounding countryside for a long time, but a lapse of 42 years was too long a period to recollect any details. They entered the house of Terezija Dremelj and her nephew Rudi with his family. There was no more doubt — they had finally reached their destination. Terezija recollected so many things that Podgoršek, in turn, translated to James. Everything fell into place. And Rudi, who was only eight years old at the time, added quite a lot of details. When Terezija placed a piece of nylon parachute on the table, the mystery was truly solved at last. Into the house on Christmas Day in 1944 had stepped James Ashley and later four other American airmen from Ashley's crew who only moments before had experienced the most dramatic event in their lives. And then suddenly, thousands of miles from their homes, they found themselves among people who received them cordially like friends and invited them to share their Christmas festivity.

Unfortunately, the events that occurred four weeks later weren't as festive. On January 21, 1945, the Germans imprisoned them in the Ljubljana castle. Fourteen days later they were transferred to a Nazi prison camp. They were finally liberated by Patton's American Army the day before VE Day (May 8, 1945).

As the Ashleys departed for the USA, they commented that they had spent seven wonderful and exciting days in Slovenia and that they would pass on their impressions to other members of the B-17 crew. They would certainly recommend that the others revisit the places in Slovenia that they had first seen in 1944.

Chapter 19

A Lucky Day at Kobarid

The events of this story occurred at Kobarid, the same place (Caporetto, Italy) that Ernest Hemingway used for a scene in his famous novel *A Farewell to Arms*. The mountainous area surrounding the small town of Kobarid has become well known because of Hemingway and the furious battles that were fought between the Austrians and the Italians. But this tale originated during World War II, and the participants of this unusual incident were the airmen of the USAAF 15th Air Force, the inhabitants of that area, and the Slovene Partisans.

At an Allied air base near Bari in southern Italy, a large fleet of bombers from the 460th Bomb Group were being readied for flight on January 20, 1945. The targets for their mission were military objectives in Lienz, Austria. Among the airmen preparing for the mission was a crew of ten under the command of their pilot, 20-year-old Lieutenant Jerry Armstrong from Ohio, near Cleveland. He was with the 15th Air Force, and this was his seventeenth mission over enemy soil. The rest of the crew — Frank Trebusak, copilot and son of Slovenian parents; navigator Roy Cooke; engineer Leo Lord; radio operator Ted N. Witkowski; bombardier Frank Diambro; and gunners Bill Petty, Elmo Gustilian, Leo Brock, and Francis Baumgartner — were also very young; most were not over 20 years of age.

They arrived at the target and had to regroup after the lead aircraft was hit; this caused them to select another target (Rosenheim). As they unloaded their bombs they came under heavy antiaircraft fire. The engineer checked for damages. Apart from the fact that they were running low on fuel, there was no evidence that they had sustained any damage. As they flew over the Adriatic at 26,000 feet, the engines began to cough — an indication that they were running out of fuel. It was necessary to return to the mainland in order to land

Jerry Armstrong (kneeling, left) and his B-24 crew at the air base in Italy. Bill Petty is standing fourth from the left.

by parachute. On a special map that they always carried, they had marked the areas that had been liberated by the Partisans. That would be where they would try to seek rescue.

Jerry Armstrong directed the aircraft toward Udine (Videm) and then Kobarid. There he gave orders to the crew to bail out while he attempted to keep the wings level. He was the last one to leave. The plane crashed into the area of the mountain Krn near the Dreznike flatlands. The pilot descended toward the snow-covered landscape and landed in snow six feet deep.

As soon as he landed, he noticed people running toward him and had the feeling that they wanted to help him. He managed to extract himself from the deep snow before they reached him. Nobody knew any English, so he could not make himself understood. Neither could he find out where he was. He only understood that it was necessary to hurry up. He was escorted to the closest farm, which was called Pri Cordiju. Until that moment he did not know what was going on around him. The underground couriers working in the area hurried to the mountain to inform the unit of local Partisans that Allied airmen had parachuted. However, the Germans from Kobarid were quicker. Before the helpless villagers, the Germans seized Armstrong and took him to the jail in Kobarid. Two of the crew members, flight engineer Leo Lord and gunner Leo Brock, were already there. They were held for two days before being taken to a prisoner-of-war camp at Nürnberg. Meanwhile, their air base in Italy had declared them missing in action. It was mid-April 1945 before Armstrong's wife, Ginny, received information from the Red Cross that he was alive. Armstrong was liberated by Patton's units on April 29 and was reunited with his wife in Ohio on May 30. The tales of some of the other crew members are related by the Partisans who rescued them.

Bogomil Hvala — Partisan name "Ivo" — was a blacksmith before the war at Slap near Kobarid. During the Fascist occupation, he was a member of the progressive organization TIGR in Primorsko (an area near the sea). The goal of this organization was to free areas of Slovenia under control of Fascist Italy. Mussolini's soldiers seized him and sentenced him to prison. At the fall of Fascist Italy in 1943, Hvala was lucky enough to be set free. He made a 400-mile trek, mostly on foot, to join the Slovenian Partisans.

He recalled the encounter with the American fliers in the following account.

* * * * *

One evening in January 1945, after four days of tough walking through six feet of snow, my comrade Janko Kranjc and I arrived at our base completely exhausted. Lying on the hay and resting, we felt we were safe as no one would search for us in such deep snow.

The next day was sunny, typical of the upper mountainous areas. At about 7:00 we heard the familiar sound of engines as we lit a fire and prepared breakfast. This sound always made the Partisans happy, for it meant that the bombers were on their way to attack Hitler's exposed flank. This time there were many of them in the air. We enjoyed watching these wonderful flocks of steel birds.

It was 1:00 when the flotilla returned after the mission was completed. The planes had barely vanished over the horizon when another plane appeared, flying low from the direction of Matajur toward Mount Krn. We knew that something was wrong with the plane, which was confirmed a moment later as we clearly saw the aircraft crash into Krn. We turned to look at the sky and saw two little dots that began to grow, which we determined to be parachutes. Two had dropped over Kobarid, two more above Matajur, and three far below us. Our chief concern was to help the stricken Allies before they fell into the hands of the Germans. For those who had dropped over Kobarid, there was no hope for rescue as a large German stronghold was located there. Our initial attempts to search for the parachutists were unsuccessful, and further searching was abandoned as night was approaching.

The next morning, all of us, including the three airmen who had spent the night hidden in a haystack, were in for a surprise. We had started a fire in front of the stable when we noticed three figures in strange uniforms at a neighbor's stable. We were convinced that they were German ski troops hunting for the fliers. I aimed my machine gun at them and shouted, "Stop! Who are you?" There was no reply, so I shouted again, "Hands up!" The closest one lifted his hands and choked out, "American!" I then knew that he was not the enemy and shouted, "Tito!" in return.

This exchange was followed by a scene that would make any film director happy. The flier came forward and embraced and kissed me. In order to further convince the strangers that we were friends, I rushed to the stable for some printed material that had the hammer and sickle displayed and showed it to them. This dispelled any doubts that they may have had, and they knew for sure that they were among friends. We invited the frozen and hungry fliers into the stable where we offered them everything that we had. One of them was of Polish extraction — Ted Witkowski — so we could communicate on a limited basis. The parents of another — Elmo Gustilian — were French, which helped a little, and the third one, Bill Petty, was American.

The rescued fliers ate, warmed themselves, and slept that night in the stable. The next morning we set out on the snowy, difficult path across Matajur to Benecija, which was the Partisan command post for Kobarid. Before we started, all three cut their chutes and wrapped them around their bodies to act as camouflage against the snowy background. The silken material also provided insulation and protection from the cold snow. These were stout fellows who had never experienced the conditions that were present at that time in the snow-laden mountains of Slovenia. With clenched teeth, two of the fliers heroically proceeded through the snow and attempted to overcome any obstacles in their path. However, Ted Witkowski had weakened, so I sent Janko ahead with the other two fliers, wrapped Ted in a tent cover, and, taking him by the legs, dragged him for hours on end over the snow; this was trying for both of us. I endured the strain due to my fitness as a blacksmith, which is a tough job.

Meanwhile, Janko had reached our destination with the two fliers and, since I was overdue, sent a Partisan patrol to come to my aid and complete the journey. When we finally arrived (I cannot recall if it was Matajur or Strmica), the natives came to the command post after learning that we had brought the Americans and prepared for a meeting that ended in a dance. Everybody wanted to see and make sure that the persons we had brought were really Americans. They were extremely excited. Prior to the dance there were some speeches on how wonderful it was to fight collectively against the common enemy — the Germans. The entire affair was risky, as the Germans could have come to this village in the mountains at any moment. Bill and Elmo came to life and were dancing with the girls from Venice. Only our Polish friend, Ted, could not come. He said that this had been the most arduous day that he had ever experienced in his life. He kept repeating this over and over.

Military representatives from the Kobarid command agreed on how to take the Americans safely and expeditiously from the town to the nearest Partisan airstrip. Both Janko and I had to return to our post. We said our good-byes and all were thankful. But the most moved was Ted, who, at parting, promised to return if he survived.

* * * * *

How the other fliers fared is remembered by Darko Ohojak from Kobarid. When he helped rescue the fliers, he was 17 years old and a political delegate at Couriers Relay Station P24B from which numerous paths and roads led all over Slovenia, including the way to the main headquarters of the Partisan Army in southern Slovenia. Today, Darko Ohojak operates a saw mill in Kobarid. He remembered his first encounter with the Americans on that day.

* * * * *

At that time the couriers moved from our old base to a stable high up in the mountains. While returning to the base on that fateful day, our attention was attracted to the sound of airplane engines. Soon afterward we saw an airplane flying low, and then we saw parachutes. We were overjoyed, as we thought that these must be the supplies sent by the Allies, since it was their practice to parachute supplies into liberated areas where there were groups of Partisans. However, we were soon convinced that people were suspended from the chutes. I watched them with my binoculars for some time and could determine quite accurately where two of them had landed. I started immediately in that direction and found the first one hidden in a deep hole that he had made in the snow. I kept asking him in both Slovenian and Italian who he was. He looked at me in amazement and finally mouthed the words "American flier." With my comrade, France Filipovic, we somehow told him that he was in safe hands and that he should wait while we searched in the vicinity for the other one.

We looked for a long time, especially in the area of the steepest slope, in the ravine, but all in vain. Just as France and I were convinced that it was all for naught, a figure arose about 50 yards away from us. We had walked by the spot and had failed to see him since he had dug into the snow and covered himself with his white parachute. The parachutist obviously didn't trust us at first, but eventually he changed his mind. He called to us and motioned with his hands for us to go to him. We had hardly arrived before he rushed forward and embraced me as tears welled in his eyes. All this was due to the fact that he saw the red star on my cap, which meant that he was among friends — the Partisans. It would be difficult for me to describe the moment when he met his buddy who had waited for us back on the path. They were extremely fortunate to meet again and be with us. One of them spoke some Croatian and Slovenian. He told us that his parents came from Yugoslavia and that his name was Frank Trebusak.

After the fliers had eaten, it was time to think about moving from the area, for the Germans at Kobarid must have determined where the fliers had landed and would be approaching the vicinity.

Ahead of us we faced a seven-hour trek across six feet of fresh snow at Matajur. We walked in snow up to our waists with utmost difficulty and hardly made any progress at all. With superhuman effort, the fliers followed in our footsteps. In no way were their clothes proper for such a hike across snowy mountains. We arrived at our destination, Benecija, late at night and exhausted before turning the fliers over to our comrades at the Kobarid command post.

Tired but satisfied that we had accomplished a good deed, we rested at a stable for a few hours. We had to regain our strength for the return trip to our courier post the next morning to assure continuity in the lines of communication.

* * * * *

Frank Trebusak 35 years later wrote a letter to the Partisans who had helped him. He wrote about the days he had spent among them:

I am extremely happy that at last I have been able to make contact with the people who helped me during the war. I will attempt to recall the incident and write about it. I was the copilot of a bomber when, in January 1945, we were returning home from action over Germany. . . . As usual, we had been briefed at our base as to where we should jump if we were to get hit. I must admit that I was afraid. However, I knew that I had a chance to survive. I guided the parachute to a soft landing in the snow in a nice mountain area. The wound from which I was bleeding was not too severe. I got myself together and began to recall what we had been told at training. I wrapped the 'chute around me to maintain warmth and then waited. I was thankful that my Slovenian parents had brought me up strong and healthy.

Fortunately, I was used to hard work and therefore able to withstand hardships. Soon I heard the sound of familiar Slovene words being spoken — "*Vstani in pridi, da te vidimo* [Stand up and come forth so that we can see you]." Overjoyed, I raised my hands into the air and approached them. I was then taken to the Partisan command post for Kobarid. The walking was hard and difficult for the snow was deep and icy, and I had to be careful not to slip and fall into a chasm. Even today I remember the snow-laden pines. I was desirous of a good meal, but it was difficult to get food. The Partisans were good — the people hardy. The Germans could not relate to the rough terrain and hard conditions — this was "guerrila" [*sic*] in the highest sense of the word.

I remember attending meetings in barracks full of flags, with pictures of Roosevelt, Tito and Stalin on the walls. First there was speechmaking which was followed with a dance. Throughout this time, the Germans were in the neighboring villages. Later, I saw burned villages — Germany's revenge for the help the people were giving the Partisans. I recall night forays by the Partisans — the woods were full of them with their supply trains and other movements. At times, shots would ring out only to be muffled by the snow. Some of the people I met at the flying field told me of having relatives in the United States of America and asked me if I would take letters to mail from Italy to the states. These requests I had to deny, for I did not want the people to have trouble in the event that I fell into the hands of the Germans.

It was early in the morning when, in the company of two Englishmen, I arrived at the airfield. From above the clouds, I heard the sound of the engines of a C-47 — it landed — we boarded and we were on the way to Italy — just like a dream — yet reality.

I am proud of the birthright given to me by my parents. With pride and thankfulness, I recall and marvel at the people who helped me. Someday when I put my affairs in order, I will come to Yugoslavia. I think that this land, apart from the good people, has a most favorable climate. I will search out the Partisans who helped me or their kin. I think that the conditions are much better for the people there today.

In concluding, I must state that the initial shock certainly ended in an interesting and fortunate manner. Also, that this type of experience helped to bring about better understanding among the peoples of the world.

I send "thanks" to all of the Partisans who helped me and especially to Darko with whom I had the initial contact after I dropped out of the sky among you!

* * * * *

As a conclusion to their story, two members of the crew of the bomber that crashed at Mount Krn — pilot Jerry Armstrong with his wife, Ginny, and Bill Petty, the gunner, with his wife, Geraldine — visited Slovenia after 30 years. I knew that they were coming to Ljubljana, the capital of Slovenia. I had previously visited the locale where they had parachuted, making unobtrusive inquiries about the dramatic events that had occurred so that I might gather as much data as possible without telling the villagers and local residents the exact date of the fliers' arrival. I did this because of my professional partiality for natural, spontaneous, candid snapshots and not for those that are planned ahead of time. In order to preserve the exclusiveness of the event, I did not give advance notice to any of my professional colleagues or even the TV studio.

The guests arrived from America and stayed at the Hotel Lev. We met one evening, and it was apparent that they were very impatient to meet the people who had intervened in their lives.

The next morning we drove out of Ljubljana. The driver was excellent, and so was his English. Our first stop was in Tolmin, where Bogomil Hvala lives. The meeting between Petty and Hvala was so touching that many of the people present wiped tears from their faces. Also present was Hvala's daughter, an English language teacher; thus we were well provided with interpreters as we continued on our way.

Next we stopped in the center of Kobarid, which was in shambles after the severe earthquake that had recently struck the Tolmin vicinity. The square at the statue of Gregorčič, a well-known Slovenian poet, was filled with local

Jerry Armstrong and his wife, Ginny, inspect a piece of his life-saving parachute during a visit to Yugoslavia.

inhabitants and other residents of the area. It was not surprising that a crowd gathered, since rumors had been spreading that some Allied Air Forces fliers might be arriving. Representatives from veterans' groups were also present as well as some who, 30 years previous, had helped the Allies in tight situations. The tragedy that happened in the air so many years before had not been forgotten.

The atmosphere at this most heartfelt meeting was spontaneous and emotional; rarely have I been at a gathering of this kind. It was this event that prompted me to gather material from similar encounters or meetings with the intention to document them in a book, which became *Stotinka Sreče*.

Fliers Jerry and Bill scanned the mountains above Kobarid through binoculars for the purpose of recalling and perhaps locating the exact spot where they had bailed out. Pilot Armstrong desired to see the building in which the Germans had imprisoned him after they had caught him in the mountains. The house was barely standing, for it had been damaged by a recent earthquake. During this time people started to bring parts of the crashed aircraft. A local resident, Frank Ursic, kept a part of the bomber's wing at home. Jerry reached out for this unusual memento as if it were a precious gift. Then Ursic and Jerry embraced, and a photo was taken of those present.

Mirko Skocir brought a smaller plated part of the aircraft, which Jerry immediately recognized as being an instrument from the bomber. As a token of gratitude, the pilot gave both of them some souvenir silver dollars that were issued at the 200th anniversary of the USA. Then another person brought metal that had been fashioned into a pan to bake cornmeal mush. Pilot Armstrong could not contain the tears in his eyes.

Then he wanted to visit the spot where he had landed by parachute, and the natives took us to a steep mountain. The nearer we came to the place, the more signs appeared to confirm that this was the spot where the tragedy had occurred.

Armstrong almost instinctively directed his steps toward the spot where he had landed in the deep snow. He stood there for a long time without uttering a word. Meanwhile, his wife bent over and picked a bunch of bluebells that abounded in the area.

The pilot remembered the place where he had buried his pistol and chute and pointed it out. He recalled hearing voices as they approached him — friend or foe? After 30 years he received the answer to the question that had bothered him all this time — how did the Germans capture him? He talked with the people who had rescued him and hidden him in one of the houses. The Germans at Kobarid had seen in which direction he had landed and rushed to the village where, after an intensive search, they located him. Cvetka, who had been turning 16, was present when they captured the pilot and cried, begging for his life. Now, after 30 years, the pilot wanted to meet Cvetka. She was standing on the threshold of her house when the group approached. She recognized him at once and exclaimed, "It is he, the right one, still as nice as he was then." Her eyes filled with tears as the wife of the pilot stepped forth and embraced her. Cvetka was so overjoyed at this meeting that she stated that she would have given her cow from the stable to have this happen. As we were leaving, Cvetka came running after us and pinned corsages of wildflowers on both the pilot and his wife. This was in memory of the joyous meeting for, until now, she was certain that the pilot was dead.

We arrived at a homestead where many B-24 parts were visible on the house. The roof was covered with aluminum; so was the door to the cowshed in front of which the guests were photographed, since the Air Forces wing insignia was still visible. Another farmer stood on the threshold of his house holding a comb made from the plane's aluminum structure.

Ex-Partisan Janko Kranjc meeting with Bill Petty.

Meanwhile, the second flier, Bill Petty, was already impatiently waiting to proceed to the place where he had bailed out. His rescuers were Bogomil Hvala and Janko Kranjc.

Bill found Kranjc, a muscular-shouldered farmer, in a field in the village of Svino at Kobarid. He was not informed about our visit, and when he noticed a group of unknown persons approaching his field, he thought they might be coming from the government to collect taxes or something of that nature.

We proceeded directly toward him. Kranjc and Bill looked at each other for a long time and then sprung into an embrace — the American businessman and the farmer from Tolmin. Interpreters had nothing to interpret — the tears and hugs of these two men said enough. We stood in the field for a long time, and then Janko invited us inside. It was then that the interpreters were quite busy appeasing the assembled people and satisfying their curiosity by relating everything that had happened during and after the war.

However, the visits were not at an end. Bill Petty wanted to visit the place where the inhabitants had offered him a safe shelter. It was the village of Livške Ravne, high up in the mountains. At that location was a modest house and a barn where Bill had spent eight days hiding from the enemy. Above all, he wanted to see the pleasant and caring mother, Amalija Paletic, who had treated him as though he were her own son. He was crestfallen when he learned that she had died two years before. The following day he arranged for flowers at her gravesite in thanks for what she had done for him.

Bill Petty and his wife, Geraldine, and a local peasant woman at Livške Ravne where the villagers hid him from the enemy.

We then went to the barn. Amalija's daughter stepped forward and opened the door for Bill and his wife. He recalled his joke of having his "Yogi-bed" here; now a heifer stood on the spot showing its wet tongue. The flier looked around the barn and remarked, "There were six head of cattle in the barn, and now I see only two." The housekeeper replied that there were still six; four of them were out in the grass pasture grazing. He told us that mother Amalija used to give him a bottle of warm milk after she milked the cows. Bill also recalled that he was awakened early in the morning by the cattle in the barn, a fact for which he was grateful, for it was in his best interest that he be awake and watch for the enemy who occasionally invaded the darkened villages with pre-dawn attacks in order to take the Partisans by surprise.

They talked about stock-farming and rural economy. It was obvious that Bill was not only an expert in airplanes but also in other matters.

Just as we were leaving the hospitable and kind villagers, we were approached by an old woman, clad in black, who offered the guests some ripe plums. When the flier tendered her a silver coin, her feelings were hurt until it was explained to her that this was a souvenir coin — then she accepted it.

Far below the village where we had parked our cars awaited another surprise for Armstrong. We were met by an unknown motorist who approached Armstrong and gave him a part of the parachute upon whose fine lines had laid the fate of the flier 30 years before. That piece of chute was carefully preserved by Roza Ivančič. When she learned that the pilot to whom the chute belonged was in the village, she took the long-treasured piece and asked Ivan Skocir to catch the pilot and give him the piece of chute to take with him to his homeland.

Then a wag from the crowd said, "If you stay with us for a day or so, the people will bring together all the missing parts of your aircraft, so you will be able to fly back to America."

Another person who joined our group was Zora Jelina, who tried to find out if anybody knew anything about the flier she had taken care of during the war. We found out that the airman was Roy Cooke from New York. While she greeted Bill and Jerry, she told us the following:

> When the Partisan couriers brought him into my house, the place was completely filled. I could hardly find a place or a hole for him to hide in. He was a good and grateful fellow. There was no other food except beans, and he would not touch them. He would rather starve than eat beans. But he did eat any other food offered. He was brought to us after an entire day's walk in the deep snow and fell asleep at once. The evening passed and the light of another day began to fade as night approached once more, but he did not come out of his den. I went to see if anything was wrong with him or if he was even dead. But everything was okay. He was just sleeping soundly. Oh, how I long to see that boy. Tell him, if you see or write to him, that I expect him.

Taking leave of the guests from the States in a pleasant inn in Kobarid, we proposed a toast wishing other crew members would also visit these places. Present at the parting was the well-known Partisan reporter Andrej Pagon ("Ogarev"), who said, "We, Tito's Partisans, fought on land — you, American fliers in the air, together for the same goal — liberty, peace, and brotherhood on earth. May these times through which we lived never be repeated again."

Before their departure from Ljubljana, the guests proclaimed that the day had been for them the second most fortunate day of their lives — the first had been January 20, 1945.

Chapter 20

American Airmen and a "Mute Farmhand"

This unusual story started on Easter Sunday, April 1, 1945, barely a month or two before the end of World War II.

Helena Debelak, the mistress of the farm Pri Slamniku (literally "At the Straw Hat" — the family name of the farm) at Lovnik near Poljčane, was swamped getting the Easter dinner ready at noon while her husband, Tone, was absorbed in reading the newspaper.

Suddenly, their 16-year-old son Janko rushed in with the news that a stranger was standing on the hillock behind their house. The man was signaling that he wanted something but would not descend any closer.

Strangers were to be approached with the utmost caution in that period of uncertainty during the war. Although it was apparent that the war would soon end, the Gestapo used all sorts of strategies to expose sympathizers or members of the Liberation Front. Thus, the farmer stepped outside to investigate the cause of his son's excitement.

Before him stood a man approximately 30 years old, tired and scared. The head of the house invited him in and discovered that the stranger was an American who had shortly before bailed out of a disabled warplane. The man could not describe any information regarding his sudden appearance due to the language barrier.

The airman accepted his hosts' hospitality and sat down, sharing the Easter dinner with the family. After eating, he indicated that he would like to wash up and hide from the Germans. Later, Tone escorted him to an old house a few hundred yards from the main road where he could hide in a small room upstairs.

Helena Debelak in front of her home on the farm where the American airman William Franklin was hidden for months.

However, the Debelaks were apprehensive as columns of enemy soldiers, retreating from the Balkan battlefields, constantly passed right by their house. Therefore, Tone decided to inform the nearest Partisans, soldiers of the Kozjansko Commando Intelligence Center, of their guest.

In turn, the Partisans needed to find someone who could converse with the airman in his language. That task was entrusted to a not-quite 16-year-old girl, Jovita Jančič (later Jovita Podgornik), nicknamed Mravljica (meaning "a small ant" — everybody agreed that she was always as busy as one, and the name stuck). Years later, when I finally ended my search and located Mravljica, she reminisced and told the remainder of the story.

* * * * *

That was not my first encounter with Allied airmen. On November 9, 1944, Anton Lah ("Zmago"), the commander of courier station 2, called me as a result of an unusual "visit" at his station by a group of American airmen. Their heavy bomber had been shot down near Maribor, and they had parachuted into the Pohorje forest.

The intelligence post was a humble hut in the vicinity of a church of pilgrimage. When I stepped into the warmly heated "house" — in Styria, the largest room of a dwelling is called a house — I caught sight of five or six tall men in beautiful uniforms and impossible shoes, quite unsuitable for walking through our wooded trails. I addressed them in English, the way I had been taught by my teacher, Mr. Nebe, who had been schooled in Oxford, England. You can imagine their surprise and joy when they discovered that they could converse with someone in their own language.

After we had pinpointed our location on a map that they produced, one of the questions was, "Where are the Germans right now?" They were greatly surprised when I showed them the Maribor-Zidani railway bridge just below our position. We could see a German patrol walking toward Poljčane quite distinctly when the airmen used binoculars. They were not in the least enthusiastic about their situation with the enemy so close to the house. We assured them that sometimes the courier post was close to the enemy for tactical reasons, as they do not expect the Partisans to be nearby. The airmen then became involved in a long discussion about being relocated to the Dolenjska region in the south. During the question and answer period, the mistress of the farm placed a large bowl of fruit on the table for our collective use. The airmen appreciated the change from the chocolates and tinned food that they had carried in their trouser pockets located below their knees.

It was dusk before we finally headed for my aunt's house, where I stayed from June 1944 until the liberation. My mother also resided there unless she was in Ptuj working as a member of the underground movement. After a short stop at our place, they, together with a group of Greeks who had fled the Germans, continued on toward the next courier post.

Later, in the middle of the night, we heard a knock on the gutters. This was a signal that we had prearranged with the Partisans. They had returned because the river had risen earlier that evening and they were not able to cross. Walking through the rain in cold and nasty weather was bad enough, but one of the airmen had also fallen into a pool of liquid cow manure and stunk to high heaven. Since there was no running water in the entire village, we had to fill buckets and haul them into the kitchen where the water was heated on a stove. Like in the "old times," the airman took a bath in a large wooden tub now normally used for washing the linen. I washed all of his underwear and outer garments. I also learned about nylon cloth, which was unknown to me before then. My mother gave him her husband's suit. The airmen were also anxious to obtain proper shoes, since they were quite helpless walking in their flying boots.

In the meantime, my mother showed the airmen a sofa and a bed in an adjoining room, while our neighbors housed the Greeks for the night. We did not sleep at all. We were used to sleepless nights as nighttime was the most appropriate time for moving about.

Our guests slept through the morning; in the meantime, their clothes had been dried and ironed. Mother brought in a good home-cooked lunch, and the boys ate enthusiastically. Meanwhile. I was occupied interpreting for them. I remember that we talked of "The Third Front," the invasion that should have been conducted in Istria. The airmen were also interested in our underground. They wondered at our organization and the cooperation of the civilians with the resistance movement.

The time for our parting was nearing. I was given soft brown gloves and a scarf with a map on it for remembrance, plus the addresses of all of the airmen. Unfortunately, all of these things were lost when an aunt of mine, fearing a police search, threw everything into the fire.

For good luck, I picked late-autumn violets that grew behind our house and pinned a bunch on each of the airmen's one-piece flying suits, as is the ancient Slovene custom.

* * * * *

Jovita then described her second encounter with an Allied airman.

* * * * *

On a sunny day, a young boy (I don't remember who he was) informed me that they had an American in the house and that they needed me as an

Jovita Podgornik ("Mravljica"). Her knowledge of English played an important part in helping rescue Allied airmen.

interpreter. I did not question where the information had come from, as I was convinced that it was "our man" who had been sent to the "right house," as we would say today. Also at my aunt's house that day were some members of the liberated town committee of Smarje pri Jelsah, and they agreed that I should visit the American airman and that they would await my return. Somebody advised me to take an empty basket so that if I had to hide anything, I could put something like potatoes over the object.

The roadway leading to the crossroad was initially uphill before descending to the village of Lovnik. As soon as the road swept gently downhill, I saw large groups of German soldiers obviously resting at the roadside, cooking for themselves and preparing to continue on their way toward Poljčane, Rogarška Slatina, and Celje. Their weapons were nested in the shape of a pyramid. Horses were grazing in the soft grass, the sun was warm, and it seemed that no one had a care in the world about the war. And so it happened that I was peacefully walking with my empty basket past all of these tired-looking men who seemingly had been fed up with everything for a long time.

In the middle of Lovnik, at the turn for the Debelaks, a young German soldier or non-com or something addressed me. (Actually, I had never been interested in the various military ranks.) He wanted to know where I was going and why I was alone in the country where "bandits" were swarming all around. He soon found that I had a good command of German, but I told a lie that I was a student and was suffering from TB, so the reason for staying in this remote area at my aunt's was to recover from my long illness. I had a forged medical certificate purchased in exchange for fresh meat in Maribor. Unfortunately, I did not have it with me that day, but I did have an excuse, and the soldier, who was young and kind, believed me. He insisted that I see him when I returned from my friend's house.

I eventually arrived at the Debelaks, who had been waiting for me. The farmer took me to a building with a small room where the American was sitting on a bed. As a young girl, having ideas and feelings remote from experience and real life (that is, given to romance), I was not in the least enthusiastic over the meeting with the American, for my first encounter with Allied airmen remained quite different in my memory. Those first boys were a little romantic, somehow ecstatic, and they fitted in with the current conception of fighters against fascism. This man, who was a little more mature than the boys, seemed to be colder, less cordial, but very curious. It was perhaps due to the fact that he had hurt his arm when his parachute had become entangled in the tree and he was in great pain. He was probably informed that I had been sent for but did not show any special enthusiasm at my arrival. I sat down on the bed beside him while the farmer stood next to us. "Are you a Partisan girl?" he asked. I answered affirmatively. Initially he wanted to know if he was safe with the farmer and if he could stay there till the end of the war. Tone, the farmer, replied with a clever suggestion: "Let him stay; he will be our mute farmhand."

The airman felt safe and relieved after I told him what the farmer had said. Maybe I was a little unjust comparing this man with the first group of fliers of last November, those on whom I had pinned violets. They were the first Americans that I had ever seen, and what I had done for them was a politically important deed. I wanted to show them that we could help people, rescue them, cook well, be hospitable, pay attention to one another. But with the

William and Beverly Franklin in their home ten years after the war ended.

American at the Debelaks, the romantic notions for an important deed were not present, for the situation was quite different, much more dangerous and risky.

As we parted, the American offered his pistol, a belt with extra cartridges, maps, and some other small military articles with which I was unfamiliar. I placed everything in the bottom of the basket, and the housewife placed potatoes on top, which made the basket quite heavy.

Let me conclude with an almost comic situation that occurred at the crossroad in the village. As soon as "my German soldier" caught sight of me, he addressed me politely and immediately offered to help me by carrying my heavy basket. To run, escape? No! A refusal? No! Taking a chance? Yes! It was safe to a point, but I still had all these fears. What if he would trip over a rock and the contents of the basket would roll out? What if . . . if . . . if . . . ?

He carried my basket as far as the crossing where the road turns to Beli Potok; he was not allowed to leave the main road. He also told me that they intended to proceed toward Slovenska Bistrica — Windisch Feirstritz, in German — at 2:00 p.m. Up to that point I hadn't realized that I had stayed with the American that long. I lied to the German that it was a long way to my home, although it only took me a few minutes to walk to Beli Potok. He took his leave at the bend in the road where it starts downhill.

When I returned to my aunt's house, where they were anxiously waiting for me, they asked what had happened. Proud of myself and the deed that I had accomplished, I dumped the contents of the basket on the table. On top of the potatoes appeared the "spoils of war," albeit Allied ones this time. I don't know much about guns, but I do know that the Colt was superb. It was admired by all present. Then I remember Černelič's hands as he grabbed the gun; he unbelted his own and handed it to a man in the group, saying, "This is now mine [as if it were a trophy] and what was mine is now yours."

I am relating this with some sadness because for the first time I was exposed to the "pecking order" in life. And yet, Černelič was a good man, maybe even one of the best that I have ever known.

The name of the American airman remained unknown to me for a long time. However, ten years after the war, by unbelievable means, a photograph of the airman was delivered to the Debelaks. His name was William Franklin. It is important to me that one of those rescued by us survived. At that time my part was unpretentious. The German's part was humorous. But the part played by Debelak, who is now deceased, was big because he risked losing his life while hiding the "mute" farmhand on his farm and keeping him away from the Germans who, along with the local collaborators, streamed past his farm every day as the front line continued to shrink and they marched north toward Germany. One slight error on his part and the consequences could have been fatal for him and his family. But we and the "mute farmhand" were lucky — we all survived.

Epilogue

The stories related in this book are representative of many that had happy endings for American airmen flying with the 15th Air Force during World War II. During the period January 1944 through April 1945, over 1,000 Allied personnel, mostly airmen who had been forced to crash-land or parachute from stricken aircraft, were rescued and returned to friendly control zones by the underground Partisans in Slovenia. This number included 389 British prisoners, 120 French or prisoners of other nationalities, and 303 American airmen, plus at least 200 additional Americans who were passed through Slovenia to other parts of Yugoslavia. The level of organization to support an effective evasion of the enemy ranged from armed resistance groups to local civilian inhabitants.

Actual evacuation of downed airmen and escaped Allied prisoners was accomplished through the local resistance organizations working with Allied military personnel in the occupied zones. Quoting from the last paragraph of the "Final Report of Mulberry Team," First Lieutenant John G. Goodwin reports:

> The credit for making these evacuations possible goes to the Partisans, not to the Allied Missions. Crews had a knack for coming down between the lines. Several times in XI Corps area Partisans were wounded or killed fighting to save these men from the enemy. When members of a crew were unaccounted for, searching parties would spend days combing the mountains. It was the Partisans who took these crews through enemy lines. During a crew's stay in the country, most of the food they received was of course Partisan. When medical treatment was needed, the best

available was given. Except in a few instances the crews were very well treated — they were not pampered, and they had to share the same hard life the Partisans led; but under the circumstances no better treatment could have been expected.[4]

In tribute to the heroic assistance provided by the resistance, an exhibition of artifacts, memorabilia, photographs, and other descriptive material was displayed in Ljubljana, the capital of Slovenia, commencing September 18, 1992, and coinciding with the 50th anniversary of the formation of Partisan organized resistance. It was sponsored by the Slovene War Veterans Organization (ZZB) to recognize the unselfish sacrifices endured by the rescuers so that the rescued could return to their loved ones. The exhibit might be transferred to a permanent site in the USA after the displays are shown to the Slovene public in 1993.

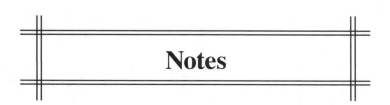

Notes

1. Among the numerous immigrants who landed on Ellis Island in 1909 was John Hribar, Sr., followed a few years later by Ivanka Zakraysek, aged 21. They were from Slovenia, Yugoslavia, and were married in 1921.

   A son was born to them in 1922 in the mining village of Krayn, Pennsylvania, where a large number of Slovenes worked. He was named after his father.

   When John grew up, he also became a miner, working the coal mines in 1939 and 1940. He also became educated, took part in sports, and enjoyed the camaraderie of his friends. In the meantime, America was drifting into World War II, and John went to work as a shipbuilder in Baltimore. After the insidious Japanese attack at Pearl Harbor, John wanted to serve America during the national emergency by enlisting in the U.S. Marine Corps Reserve. After recruit training at Parris Island, South Carolina, and basic training in North Carolina, he shipped from San Diego, California, in November 1944 to the Hawaiian islands where the 28th Regiment, 5th Marine Division was preparing for the invasion of Iwo Jima.

   He participated in that invasion from February 19 to March 2, 1945. He fought for the conquest of the slopes, and February 23 was the best day in his life as he saw the American flag being raised on top of Mount Suribachi. Eight days later he was seriously wounded. Exactly a month following, while in the U.S. Naval Hospital at Pearl Harbor, he was awarded the Purple Heart medal.

   John Hribar is now a member of the 5th Marine Division Association and a life member of Liberty Chapter No. 22 of the Disabled American Veterans.

Several years ago, after having read reports in *Prosveta,* an American publication for Slovenes, he became an active associate of the Slovene American Institute/Slovene Research Center of America, Inc., founded and directed by Professor Edward Gobetz.

2. While the article also mentions that an additional three aircraft from an adjacent element in the formation were lost due to enemy action, the official USAF report for the 98th Bomb Group states a total of three losses for April 2.

3. The Neretva is a 218-kilometer river in Herzegovina, Yugoslavia. During three months of furious fighting (December 1942-March 1943) between the Partisans and the enemy (Germans, Italians, and quislings), there were many Partisan wounded who were successfully evacuated to southern parts of the territory. A major exception was the 4th Division, which suffered heavy casualties before they finally broke through on March 16 and 17 of 1943.

The Neretva was also the site of a magnificent film starring Richard Burton in the role of the late Marshal Tito.

4. From the records of the Office of the Strategic Services No. 226, Appendix B: Evacuation of U.S. Air Crews. National Archives entry 154, box 25, folder 356.

Index

by Lori L. Daniel